CLOS
CLINO

In the same series

Easy PC
Get It Across
Think Change
Right Way to Write Reports
Presentations
Handling Publicity the Right Way

Uniform with this book

CLOSE THE SALE, CLINCH THE DEAL

Selling the Professional Way

Shaun Sheppard

RIGHT WAY

Typeset in 11/13pt Times by Letterpart Ltd., Reigate, Surrey.

Printed and bound in Great Britain by Cox & Wyman Ltd., Reading, Berkshire.

The *Right Way* series is published by Elliot Right Way Books, Brighton Road, Lower Kingswood, Tadworth, Surrey, KT20 6TD, U.K. For information about our company and the other books we publish, visit our web site at www.right-way.co.uk

CONTENTS

1

THE PROFESSIONAL SALES PERSON

I have been a salesman for the best part of twenty years and have worked with a number of top-class professional sales people in a variety of industries. This book pinpoints what makes the best sales people good and what differentiates them from the also-rans. This information will be useful to anyone, not just sales people, looking to improve their sales effectiveness in an increasingly difficult marketplace. These days just about every professional person – doctors and lawyers, architects and accountants included – will have to do some selling during their careers because business will no longer just come to them. They have to go out and find it. And there is a lot of competition.

Selling is a results-based profession – you can achieve your target or fail – and the differences between those who succeed and those who fail can be measured. Over time the best sales people will consistently out-perform everyone else. They may have to sell the same products, achieve the same targets, face the same market pressures and have similar sales territories to their colleagues. But somehow they manage to turn in above average performances year in, year out, whereas many of their colleagues struggle even to get close to their targets. By identifying and highlighting those areas where the top professionals 'gain an edge' we can all improve our sales performance.

What is selling?

Selling is such a basic part of living that we all instinctively know what it is, but trying to find a concise definition that covers all the activities of the professional sales person is tough. Here is my stab at it:

Selling is the process of establishing trust in your ability to recommend a solution to customers' needs or desires and helping them to invest in your recommendations.

It may require perseverance in drawing people's attention to something new – something they were not aware of might be of value to them. It will certainly involve negotiation, discussion, and persuasion. Listening, questioning, empathy and understanding will all be necessary too. But, ultimately, selling is all about helping customers to make a purchasing decision which is right for them.

In some senses it is easier to define in terms of what it isn't. For me, professional selling is definitely **not** about coercing people into buying things they don't need or want. We all like to think that we are astute and capable of seeing the wool being pulled over our eyes, but that is not always the case. It is possible to hoodwink or bamboozle people into buying just about anything because people buy from people. If people like and trust a sales person, they will often overlook or ignore anything dubious or uncertain. They will accept what he says at face value. There's a fair chance that you have done this too, and on more than one occasion. I know I have!

Even the best-intentioned sales people can cause confusion sometimes. That's why many contracts, particularly for financial services, now have 'cooling off' clauses so that the customers can reconsider the purchase in the cold light of day and cancel if they feel uneasy. But the fact remains that people buy from people they trust, like or, in some cases, fear, and the unscrupulous can exploit this. That is why selling is often seen as a dirty word. Given pension mis-selling scandals, dubious 'home improvement' sales people and rogue secondhand car dealers, it is easy to see why. To me, these 'sales people' are not trying to sell anything. They are just trying to con people. They are looking only to make one order out of the punter; to off-load something (often dodgy) as quickly as they can, take the money and then either run or deny any responsibility for the results.

Professional selling is not about exploitation or rip offs and this book is not concerned with the unethical, the unprincipled or the unprofessional. Professional sales people understand that long-term relationships are the key to lasting success: which means acting ethically and with integrity. They know that the easiest way to sell is not just to people who have already bought from them, but to people who were happy with what they bought and comfortable with the whole sales process. And that is what professional selling is all about – helping the customer to make a decision that is right for him. This is true even in those sales positions where you are only likely to make one-off sales, like retail. Selling as if you were expecting to develop a long-term relationship is still the key to success – who knows if that customer might come back for more at some time? And he might well recommend you to others.

Why do we need professional sales people?

Buying and selling are two of the most basic processes in society – we all bargain and barter, buy and sell on a daily basis. Yet, just as we can all kick a ball around in the park on a Sunday, and perhaps exhibit some natural skill or talent, it doesn't mean we qualify as professional footballers. The difference between the amateur sales person and the professional is just as great. If selling was as simple and easy as playing park football, everyone would be doing it, earning large salaries, and every business would be prosperous. The reality is different. Professional selling is complex,

Yet, just as we can all kick a ball around in the park on a Sunday . . .

demanding and unremitting. It is no good just diving in at the deep end in the hope that you will quickly learn to swim. Today's marketplace demands that sales people are properly trained, experienced and dedicated to the job and if they are not, they will sink without trace. Here are eight reasons why the job is a difficult one:

1. Customers and buyers are increasingly sophisticated, well trained and perceptive. They know what they want and can make considered judgments on value and cost, features and benefits, because they have much greater access to information than at any time in the past.
2. Customers have greater choice in where they can source their requirements than ever before and can change suppliers easily if there is any hint of a better price, specification, service, long-term relationship and so on. Loyalty to one preferred supplier is a thing of the past.
3. The competition, both at home and abroad, is intelligent, well trained and aggressive. There is only so much business there to get and everyone wants to

maximise their share. They will be queuing up to take your customers or beat you to a sale if you fail to deliver or take your eye off the ball.

4. Technology affects all businesses and the increasing speed of change means that new products, services, markets and opportunities need to be grasped and addressed as soon as they emerge. Just keeping up is no longer good enough.

5. Business is increasingly global and is characterised by mergers and buy-outs, bankruptcies and takeovers. Shareholder pressure means that for any business to survive long term, it needs to sell as much as possible, as profitably as possible, to the widest possible number of customers. And it must hang onto those customers for as long as possible.

6. The speed of change and the sheer amount of information available makes it impossible to keep abreast of everything. Having your finger on the pulse of what really matters is vital.

7. Even in the most successful company, resources are scarce. The ability to attract those resources to your opportunities is essential.

8. Selling is about people and because people are involved in the process, both buyers and sellers, the unexpected can and will happen. There is no magic formula to guarantee success every time.

Yet, conversely, the same reasons that make the sales person's job a difficult one also mean that a professional sales force is essential for any company wishing to compete successfully in their chosen marketplace. Without competent sales people, a business will fail to keep up in the race to increase profitability and market share. It will miss new opportunities and lose customers to more capable competitors. I know some people will debate the point, but selling is the basis of all business.

Unless an order is taken, nothing needs to be produced, delivered or invoiced. And that means that professional sales people, who can bring in the business regardless of the pressure, will always be in demand.

Is selling the career for you?
A career in sales is great fun. It definitely isn't easy in today's demanding marketplace, but, in terms of job satisfaction, financial reward, career advancement and personal gratification, selling seems to be one of the few professions that can deliver it all. That is not to say it is without its frustrations, but the benefits far outweigh the negatives. However, a job in sales isn't for everyone and I have seen people give it a try only to be put off by a wide range of factors such as:

- Selling can be lonely.
- Competition and pressure, deadlines and targets are involved.
- Money is at stake and a large part of your earnings depend on commission rather than salary.
- People are integral to the process and some of them can be difficult and hard to manage.
- Rejection can be a constant companion.
- You have to find the motivation and inner strength to pick yourself up after setbacks.
- Although you may be part of a team, the responsibility for success lies with the sales person.

Yet, for some people, these factors are the very reason why they relish the challenge of a sales career and enjoy it so much, because:

- They like the independence.
- They thrive on pressure because they are competitive by nature.

- They have the direct ability to influence how much they
  can earn.
- They like people and are genuinely interested in them,
  even the difficult ones.
- They never take no for an answer.
- They are optimistic and expect success despite current
  problems.
- They like the responsibility.

Those of us who thrive in a demanding environment, and who
relish responsibility and challenges, have the potential for a
long-lasting and lucrative career. It gives us the freedom to be
our own boss while still benefiting from the security of a large
company environment. It involves travel, independence and
variety – no two days are ever the same. We get to meet
people from all sorts of backgrounds, at many different levels,
and can gain an insight into how different markets and
businesses operate. It is potentially financially well rewarded
and is one of the few employment options where age, race and
sex are increasingly immaterial. It is also an excuse to have a
good time and I have yet to meet a great sales person who
didn't have a sense of humour, or a sales team who didn't
know how to let their hair down occasionally.

What type of career?
Good sales people are always in short supply and if you are an
achiever, whether you are just starting work, returning to it or
are already employed, there will be no shortage of career
opportunities open to you. Just about any line of business you
care to mention will need a sales person in some capacity or
other and here are a few choices:

1. **Telephone Sales**.   There are two types of telesales person,
Inbound and Outbound. Inbound sales people take enquiries
over the phone and turn them into orders. They rarely use the

phone to look for customers. Typically, mail order companies will use inbound sales people and they may also be coupled with a general customer service facility. Outbound sales people use the phone as a cold-calling and canvassing tool, typically using a list of target phone numbers and a calling script to look for customers. Outbound telesales can be very demanding, especially if you handle rejection poorly, but it is used increasingly in a wide range of industries.

2. **Internal Sales.** Typically these sales people are in areas like retail, car sales, estate agencies and so on, where they meet the general public but rarely, if ever, have to search for business out in the field. It may involve some telesales and there will be a need for good people-handling skills, but, on the whole, the customer comes to the sales person rather than the other way round.

3. **Field Sales.** Field sales people go out and look for customers (always business customers rather than the general public) in a territory or patch. They may have leads to work from and some existing customers to call on, but they will also have to prospect for new customers and manage their territory – in person and on the phone. They will be expected to find business rather than having it brought to them. This type of sales role is common to virtually all types of industry or marketplace.

4. **Direct Sales.** Direct selling refers to sales people who sell directly to the public and is used extensively in industries like insurance, pensions, home improvements, and so on. The sales person will probably have a number of existing customers to manage and may well be supplied with leads, but will also have to cold call and use the telephone to find new opportunities. Typically, calls will be made on people at home, so the hours may be at odds with normal working practice.

5. **Indirect Sales.**   Indirect selling is a form of business to business (i.e. not to the public) selling where the sales person sells goods or services to another manufacturer, dealer or supplier for them to sell on to the marketplace. Dealer Sales, OEM (Original Equipment Manufacturers) Sales, VAR (Value Added Reseller) Sales, Partner Sales, selling to wholesalers and even selling to retailers could all be classed in this category. Usually the sales person will have a number of defined accounts to manage, but searching for new business may also be involved. In some cases, these positions can be very senior, although the basic function is just the same as for any other sales role. Inevitably, the companies they are dealing with will have sales people too and the job may entail joint-working with them; perhaps in an advisory, consultative or training capacity, as well as straight selling.

6. **Sales Engineers and Sales Consultants.**   Typically these are more specialised selling roles where the sales person needs specific technical or market knowledge in order to work with clients and prospects. For example, I once worked for a company selling complex control systems to power stations. Most of the salesmen were Sales Engineers who understood in detail the engineering and technical problems of their customers because they had been engineers before they became sales people. The basic functions are identical to other sales roles.

7. **Consultative Selling, Strategic Selling, Major Account Sales.**   These are just some of the titles applied to what the recruitment consultants call 'big ticket opportunities' – sales positions where the opportunities are very important to the sales company's growth plans, often large, usually complex and can take months (occasionally years) to sell. This is where you will find many senior professional sales people. Experience, knowledge, maturity and the ability to work at Board level within their customers are prerequisites in this sort of

sales role. Typically, the sales person is positioned as a solutions provider and partner, but, ultimately, the actual sales skills required are little different from those needed elsewhere.

8. New Business versus Account Management.   New business selling is all about opening up brand new accounts from scratch. It involves cold-calling, prospecting and tenacity. Account Management means managing existing accounts or customers so that they not only continue to buy from you, but also buy more. It is all about developing long term relationships.

Some people make a very clear distinction between these two functions – Hunters and Farmers – with the emphasis on Hunters as being the most desirable. Personally, I don't see the difference as being quite that cut and dried (or that derogatory – Hunters as active 'go getters' and Farmers as passive 'order takers') and nearly all of the roles outlined above need a mix of the two in order to be successful. Opening up new accounts from scratch is a very real skill and it is essential for continued growth. But managing existing accounts is also important because it is much easier and more cost effective to sell to a customer who is already buying from you. And, if you get it wrong, there are plenty of competitors waiting to snatch your customer away. A sales person may specialise in one or the other function, but I feel that the truly well-rounded should be able to do both. Inevitably, though, many companies see New Business Development as of particular importance and a premium is often placed on this ability.

9. Commodity Selling versus Solutions Selling.   There can be a lot of snobbishness in selling. On the one hand, solutions selling, i.e. large bespoke deals tailored for individual customers and negotiated over long timescales, is often seen as the pinnacle of a sales person's aspirations. Commodity sales on the other hand – the selling of day to day, lower value items *en* *masse* – can often look like the humdrum end of the profession; a place where juniors cut their teeth. The reality is that both types of selling are needed in the marketplace and professional selling skills are just as relevant in both. It is true that many sales people gravitate from commodity to solutions selling as their careers develop, but I know others who are very happy 'piling it high and selling it cheap' and make a good living at it. They like the immediacy and short term targets and, although they have to sell a lot of products to earn a good salary, they are motivated by the challenge. The skills required in commodity selling can also be a little different from those in solutions selling. Although trust and relationships are important, the commodity sales person may only have one chance to close an order – in his first meeting with a prospect. In solutions selling, relationships are often developed over many meetings and an attempt to close at the first meeting can actually be detrimental.

10. **Big Deals versus Little Deals.**   Some sales people only go out and look for the 'big deal,' chanting one of the old sales clichés like a mantra: "It's as easy to close a big deal as a small one" or "Small deals often cause more trouble than they are worth". Like all clichés, they do contain some truth but to pursue big deals at the expense of all small ones is a crime. It is also something that most sales people cannot afford, yet I have seen colleagues hang out all year for the deal that will fulfil their target in one go and ignore perfectly good smaller opportunities in the process. They invariably fail. Big deals by their vary nature are unpredictable and rarely come in on time – if they come in at all. Their size attracts a lot of competition. Conversely, there are sales people who are uncomfortable with big deals. They are frightened of the potential risks, and even the rewards, and stick to the small and safe. They inevitably fail too. You have to close a lot of small deals to make a big target. Top

professionals will evaluate every opportunity on its merits and will have a mix of big and small deals on the go at any one time. They will not limit themselves to a certain type of opportunity. They know that some big deals will be so time-consuming that they are just not worth attempting, and that some small deals could well lead to bigger and better things in the future.

What's in a title?

One of the things that has always amused me about selling is the lengths many companies go to in order to disguise the fact that their sales people are indeed sales people. Client Managers, Relationship Directors, Business Development Executives, District Managers – job titles often bear little or no relation to the real function performed. This has developed partly because of the fear that 'sales representative' smacks a little too much of those door to door commercial travellers of old, and partly to give the position more gravitas so that it will be easier to make contact with customers at a higher level. The reality is that *any* sales person has the right and the personal authority to talk to anyone at a customer organisation. From the Managing Director to the office cleaner, the sales person should feel comfortable and at ease with anyone he sees, because any form of contact with the customer can be valuable. There is an understandable reticence, especially among younger sales people, to talk to senior figures at their customers' company. But if you have something valuable to say and can demonstrate that you will not waste their time, directors and senior managers will see you. Gravitas comes from you, personally, not from your job title.

On a different note, titles are often used to denote grades or levels of experience, especially in larger companies, and it can demonstrate that a proper career structure is in place. For example, a career progression from junior to senior selling roles can be seen in the following specific job titles:

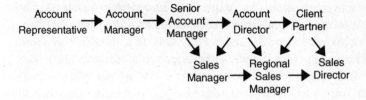

In this example, there is a clear promotion path from the newly recruited Account Representative to the Account Manager, through Senior Account Manager to the Account Director and finally on to the most senior level of pure sales position, sometimes called the Client Partner. None of these positions has any direct man-management responsibility and there is an understanding in the industry that some people want to see their careers develop and their responsibilities increase without the need to start line managing people. However, a move into sales management is something many sales people aspire to and as you gain experience, there are opportunities to move into management at many levels. The diagram shows how pure sales positions and man management positions overlap and how people might make the move as their career develops.

It is as well to be aware that each company also has its own conventions regarding job titles. When I first started out in selling I was basically a sales rep. looking after a geographic territory but, because I was managing sales in a region, my title was the much grander Regional Sales Manager.

Titles can also denote a particular market sector or type of selling – Software Sales Executive, Pharmaceutical Sales Representative, Local Government Account Manager, Retail Sales Manager, Finance Sector Sales – the list is endless. Look in any of the quality papers that contain job advertisements and you will see that many positions require specific abilities, product knowledge or market experience and that you will be ruled out if you don't have them. To a certain extent this is to be expected. Knowledge, contacts and experience are valuable commodities and any company seeking to recruit additional staff wants to capitalise on them. They want sales people to be effective as soon as they start, rather than having them spend time finding out who to speak to and what market issues are of particular importance. However, there is a tendency to pigeon-hole people, especially by recruitment consultants, and I think there is a case to be made that good sales people can make the transition between different markets and products very effectively. Of course they can't sell anything to anyone, but selling is more about enthusiasm than anything else. If you really believe in the product you are selling and can transmit that enthusiasm to your customers, you will be successful, regardless of your past experience. Unfortunately, convincing some recruitment consultants and employers can be an uphill struggle.

What makes professional sales people professional?

Great sales people are not just professional, they are outstandingly good at what they do. The sales person's key function is to bring in orders. And top professionals consistently bring in more and better business than anyone else. Pareto's Law (a scientific principle which calculates that 80% of your results will come from 20% of your effort) demonstrates that the top 20% of sales people will generate around 80% of the orders a company takes. It doesn't mean that the other 80% of the sales force are not professional or that the business they win is somehow less valuable. But what it does mean is that the top 20% are outstandingly successful. And they have a tendency to operate at this level consistently.

It is probably fair to say that outstanding sales people are born, not made. Fortunately, the characteristics that make them so outstanding can be identified and we can all learn from them, whatever capacity we hope to sell in. They are not godlike figures moving in mysterious ways – although to some of the also-rans it may seem like this – nor are they exceptionally lucky or particularly intelligent. Top professionals are human just like the rest of us, but what sets them apart are a number of key attributes – attributes we all possess in some measure or other already – which, when combined and tuned for optimum performance, become a highly effective tool for closing business:

1.   It may be a cliché but in order to be a professional sales person you need to look, think, act and talk like one. And you need to do this with everyone you meet in the course of business. Not just your customers, but within your own company, with your business partners and any suppliers or third parties you might work with. Professionalism is a state of mind that must permeate every aspect of your business life.

2.   The best sales people plan to be successful. They know what they want out of their careers, as well as life in general, and they intend to achieve it. They work out what steps they have to take in order to get to where they want to be. Problems and setbacks are hurdles to overcome rather than barriers to success. Professionals know the value of time and plan to make the best use of it. They do not waste their own or anyone else's time and are respected for this. They also have the ability to focus on the task in hand – to concentrate solely on what they are doing and not allow external distractions to interfere.

3.   Top sales people work hard. They do that little bit more than everyone else. They may make it look easy, but the effort they put in will come as a revelation to the also-rans. Productivity is part of the process, but so is 'thinking smart' – knowing the best places to spend time and effort in order to achieve the greatest results. Preparation is also key and the very best professionals try and leave nothing to chance. They know that luck is not a

factor in success. It is too unreliable. But it is possible to 'make your own luck' – as Arnold Palmer the golfer once said, "It's funny, but the harder I practise, the luckier I get" – and top sales people practise being successful.

4.   Top sales people are very comfortable with themselves. They enjoy what they do and cope with the pressures, rarely transmitting them to their customers or colleagues. They are professional, but relaxed; at ease dealing with the receptionist or the chief executive as the circumstances demand. Their confidence in their ability to deliver encourages trust and builds strong relationships.

5.   They have the right attitude. They believe in what they sell and are enthusiastic, transmitting this enthusiasm to their customers. They are optimistic by nature and believe they will be successful, which makes them highly resilient, able to bounce back after setbacks and remotivate themselves. They are very competitive and, while this may be masked by a relaxed and easygoing persona, they have a deep seated need to win. Playing the game may be fun, and they certainly relish the thrill of the chase, but victory is the key driver. They demonstrate integrity in everything they do and endeavour at all times to do what they say they will do.

6.   The most successful sales people close more business than anyone else. They know that bringing in the business is their key responsibility and everything they do is focused on this aim. However, the desire to win does not blind them to the need to be sensitive and flexible and to address each sales opportunity on its own merits. They know that no two opportunities are ever the same and that a successful outcome will only be achieved if they listen carefully and then react accordingly. They make sure that they have the widest possible selection of tools available to them to help them close rather than restrict-

ing themselves to just one or two. Professional sales people make it easy for customers to buy and they help customers make the right decisions for themselves.

7.   They know that people are the key to success and that you will sell nothing if you cannot accept this. People are unpredictable by nature and the ability to manage them and work with them is a prerequisite. Professionals are interested in people and accept them as they are. They don't waste time wishing 'so and so' were less obstructive, they work around him; they try to understand why 'such and such' is antagonistic so that they can neutralise his objections. Selling is all about relationships, trust and respect, and whether they are working as part of a team or on their own, professional sales people seek to get the best out of everyone they meet – customers, colleagues, partners and associates.

8.   Top sales people never stop looking for new business opportunities. They are entrepreneurial by nature; inquisitive and interested. Selling is more a way of life for them than just a job and, while many of them can switch off and relax away from the office, their interest in what is happening around them means that they are constantly filing information away which may be useful in some future business context. A constant source of new business is essential to long term success and the best professionals know that it is no good closing one piece of business if there aren't several others following on behind – one-offs are just not good enough. Prospecting is a continuous activity and if you close, on average, one order out of every three pieces of business you bid for, every order must be replaced with at least three new prospects. Only the very best sales people ever achieve this.

2

THE SALES PROCESS

What is the sales process?
For most sales people, whether they are selling big complex deals or commodity products, there are procedures – a routine if you like – that need to be followed in order to fulfil all of the obligations of a professional sales person. It starts with the process of finding customers and managing a territory, through developing a pipeline and maintaining an accurate forecast, to closing deals and ensuring that orders are fulfilled properly. It includes being able to present your products and services effectively, keeping your knowledge and skills up to date, getting appointments with customers, running meetings properly, keeping records, and so on. Professional sales people know that each part of the process is important and, even if it seems time-consuming or mundane, they work through it thoroughly. To skip any part of the process or to complete it poorly will lose you business in the long run.

The sales process includes the following key activities: Planning, Prospecting, Meeting Prospects, Questioning, Presenting, Quoting, Closing, Delivering, Account Management, Training, Forecasting and Record Keeping. These could appear to have a loose order, but in reality they are not consecutive – some activities will depend on others and sales people will be doing all of these all of the time if they are doing the job properly. For example, no sales person will wait until he has closed an order to start prospecting; prospecting is a continuous process. Some of these topics are detailed enough activities to warrant their own chapters: Chapter 3 – Planning, Chapter 5 – Closing, and Chapter 9 – Training. The remaining steps in the sales process are covered in detail below. All are important.

Prospecting for new business

You will always need a constant source of new and viable business, regardless of how successful you are. Unless you are incredibly fortunate, you will not find a flood of orders in the post or the phone constantly ringing with people wishing to buy from you. You will have to go out and find new opportunities for yourself. Some sales people worry unduly about where their business will come from. The reality is that there are many sources.

1. The first and easiest source of new business is from existing customers. They are already familiar with your company and, assuming service has been all they desired, they will be receptive to approaches for new or additional business. Never forget to widen your circle of contacts within an existing customer. Not only will it help you to develop your long-term relationship, you may also discover whole new areas that you can sell into.

    Your existing customers can also make suggestions (and don't be afraid to ask) about potential prospects you can approach. In some cases, they might even recommend that one of their own partners, suppliers or associates, should get in contact with you. This may be rare, and it certainly depends on the level of service you provide to the existing customer, as well as the relationship you have with them, but it does happen. I secured a very nice order from a medium sized retailer in this way.

My biggest customer, who was providing the retailer with consultancy services, suggested the retailer contact me because, if their experience was anything to go by, my products would save him money. There was nothing in it (on the face of it) for my major customer, but it certainly ensured that I continued to give them the very best service I could and went out of my way to help them out if they had problems.

2. Maintain a list of prospects who may have been interested in what you had to say but were not in a position to buy at the time. Also a list of all those people you contact who said, ''No, not at the moment, thank you''. People's requirements change, new buyers join, fresh money becomes available – nothing is static in business and, unless you are 100% sure your products and services are definitely inappropriate for a particular company, there is no reason to take 'no' as a permanent answer. Your company is also likely to have a list of people who have inquired about goods and services in the past, or to whom quotations have been made but never followed up – even old customer lists – these can be a good source of leads, but don't rely on them solely. Make a couple of calls a day to see if they are still in the market, but don't spend all your time on them.

3. National and local newspapers, as well as the trade press, often contain articles on new companies opening up in your area, or carry advertising from companies you didn't know about. I used to sell advertising space many years ago and we often trawled through the business press to see who was currently advertising on the basis that, as they were already spending money on advertisements, they might be more susceptible to an approach from us. Job ads are a valuable source of market information and contacts, and are also a good way to see if your existing customers, or even your competitors, are

expanding and taking on staff. Trade directories, business telephone directories, advertising hoardings, lorries and vans can all be useful sources of contact information. The Internet is also increasingly useful in this respect and a vast amount of information is now easily accessible. And never forget to spread your business card around as much as possible. I must confess that I have never received a call from a potential customer just because they happened upon my card, but colleagues tell me it does happen, particularly in markets like personal finance where satisfied customers often pass your card onto friends and acquaintances.

4. Do not underestimate the value of networking. Contacts are the stock-in-trade of sales people and keeping in touch with old customers and colleagues can be a valuable source of new business leads. Many sales people join trade associations, clubs or societies in order to keep their ear as close to the ground as possible. The opportunity to speak at a trade association event can be invaluable in gathering new leads and contacts. For example, a friend of mine who sells financial services kept in touch with another friend from school who became a chartered accountant. The accountant was organising a local area meeting of the Institute of Chartered Accountants and invited our friend to give a talk on the benefits of independent financial advisors. The talk was well-received and our friend secured a couple of good contacts who later referred clients to him for pensions and other financial services advice.

5. Your current business partners and associates can often be a valuable source of leads, especially if you are in the habit of passing leads on to them. It is also common practice for alliances to form in order to address particular business opportunities, and companies who might be rivals in some circumstances decide to co-operate in

others because the mix of products and services might be right for a specific opportunity. For example, a software provider, hardware vendor and a consultancy services company might team up to address a large opportunity which none of them could tackle on their own. In other circumstances they might team up with different companies and engage in active competition with the very people they partnered with on a previous deal. This is sometimes called Co-opertition (co-operation/competition) and is very common in some markets. Leads can be generated by any of the partners and by demonstrating your willingness and ability to work in this way, good quality sales opportunities can sometimes be brought to you; opportunities of which you might previously have been unaware.

6.   Your company will almost certainly be engaged in some form of advertising or marketing and this can be a valuable source of leads or contact information. Direct mail is notoriously inefficient with a less than 2% response rate, however even those few returns are usually very valuable. Some companies use telesales teams to generate leads for sales people to follow up, and many companies exhibit at conferences, trade fairs and exhibitions, all of which can generate leads or contacts. The whole area of e-Commerce or e-Business is developing rapidly and if your company has a website, make sure you use it effectively to generate leads and contact information.

7.   Many sales people I know set up their own seminars targeted at specific customers or business requirements. I found it a very useful technique when I was selling computers to local government – there were so many changes in legislation that computer systems were needed in many new areas. I set up seminars with guest speakers who specialised in the new legislation and I

Direct mail is notoriously inefficient . . .

invited the management team of those departments affected. The response was always excellent – often oversubscribed – because the subject matter and the target audience were specifically matched. It never failed to generate a number of good quality leads, as well as plenty of good contacts and useful background information about the market in general. I made several sales using this approach. It is worth noting, however, that planning and setting up this kind of event is very time-consuming (sometimes costly) and should only be used sparingly, otherwise the effort involved will detract from your normal activities.

8. One tip I learned early on in my career is to forward plan my diary. If a prospect tells you he will not be buying for several months, tell him you'll call back in two months' time to keep in touch and put it in your forward planner so you do not forget to follow it up. If you sell a month's supply of a particular product, tell the customer you'll call back in three weeks to pick up the re-order when

stocks get low – put it in your diary. If you sell something like life insurance, make sure you book a regular
yearly appointment with each client to review his affairs
– put it in the diary.

Use the forward planner to keep track of quotations
and follow ups, key customer holidays, dates of Board
meetings – anything which might affect the future buying process. As you work around your territory, you will
pick up so much valuable information like this that you
will forget it if you do not record it in some way. For
example, if you sell to local government, all major
purchasing decisions need to go through a tendering
procedure before being voted on or rubber-stamped by a
full council meeting – the timetable for the complete
process is a matter of public record and you should
record the key dates in your diary. It is no good forecasting a piece of business to happen on a specific date and
finding the main decision-maker is on holiday or that the
council meeting is two months away. You will end up
with egg on your face for forecasting incorrectly and
your manager will be less than amused! By keeping on
top of anything that could result in potential business in
this way, you will reduce the effort involved in prospecting in the future. There is also nothing quite so motivating as knowing you have plenty of potential business to
look forward to.

9.   When all else fails try cold calling. Knocking on doors
can be very demoralising – some sales people even see
it as demeaning – but it is a very realistic way of finding
new business. My approach has always been to make it
as easy as possible on myself and never to try and sell
anything on that first cold-call. If I am visiting an
existing customer on a trading estate or in a large office
block, making a couple of calls on adjacent businesses
is no effort and takes little time. Receptionists are well

used to sales people calling and will tell you who is responsible for buying their goods and services – if you are polite and don't interrupt their job too much. They might even find out for you if they don't know. Ask for a compliments slip so that you have the company name and address and then write the contact's name and title down, including his telephone extension number and secretary's name if possible. Leave a business card for him – it may not be passed on, but it does no harm – and then leave for your next call. When you get back to the office, call the contact up, explain that you have an existing customer almost next door and make an appointment to see him when you are next in the area. I have found this technique very successful and it avoids any immediate face-to-face rejection or awkwardness that might result from trying to see the contact on that first cold call.

Meeting the prospect

Unless you are involved in telesales, you will need to make a face-to-face appointment with your prospects if you are going to sell anything. Like Closing, getting that first appointment can seem a bit of a black art and a lot of sales people dread making those first few calls to secure a meeting with a new prospect, mainly because they are worried about rejection. I think the view that prospects (and their secretaries) will always say 'no' to sales people who call them up to arrange a meeting is a bit of a myth. Put yourself in their shoes. They probably get at least a dozen calls a day from sales people and suppliers all looking to arrange meetings. If the prospect saw them all he would do nothing else all day long. They are bound to reject anything unsuitable, ill-prepared or poorly presented, and they will be ruthless because they just don't have the time to waste. But, prospects also know that sales people are a vital source of new ideas and information and if you have something valuable to say, they will try to make the time to listen. And if they really need something, then their doors will always be open to the right approach.

In trying to get an appointment you could try the numbers game if you have the stamina. As a colleague of mine used to say, "Kiss enough frogs and you'll find a prince", meaning: make enough cold calls and someone will see you eventually. And he was right. If you persevere, you will get meetings, but it will be time-consuming and you will have to get used to hearing 'no' continually.

The professional way of getting in to see a customer is as follows:

1. Choose how you will make your first approach – by letter or telephone. Each is effective and there is no preferred option.
2. Do your preparation well in advance. Make sure you know exactly whom you need to contact and why you want to meet them. Practise how you will deliver your message.
3. Be professional. Assume the outcome will be positive in advance. Be relaxed and don't waste anyone's time. If the customer asks for literature before agreeing to a meeting, send it but tell him you will follow it up and then do so. If a secretary is acting as a barrier, ask her the most effective way of getting to your contact and then take her advice. If it doesn't work, go back and ask for her help. She is then quite likely to co-operate. Do not try and be clever. Always be polite.
4. Once you have secured the meeting, confirm it in writing, either by fax, letter or e-mail.

If you choose to send a letter as your method of first contact, remember you will still have to call later on to follow the letter up and make the appointment, but a good letter can sow the seeds of anticipation so that the prospect is already interested in receiving your call. Here are some tips on writing an effective first contact letter:

1. Make sure you know why you are writing the letter, what you are trying to say and what outcome you are hoping to achieve. Don't over complicate things and check that what you have written is indeed what you really want to say. Get someone else to read it if you are in doubt.

2. Keep it short and punchy. Don't waffle. People very rarely read more than one page of any business letter and an introductory letter should never extend beyond the first side.

3. Tell the recipient why you are writing and what you are going to do next. Don't leave it up to them to decide the next action. Make sure you do what you say you will do.

4. Include something that will be relevant to the recipient and will make them sit up and take notice. But make sure it is something you can justify and can support with background information when you meet.

5. Avoid being stuffy and try and write as you speak. Avoid humour and informality and do not use any jargon, marketing speak or acronyms.

6. Make sure grammar and spelling are correct and that you use the right names and titles. Until I have spoken to a prospect I still like to retain the formality of using their title in opening the letter – Dear Dr. Smith, or Dear Miss Jones, rather than Dear John or Dear Jenny.

7. It is a good idea not to include a brochure or leaflet at this stage because it will look like a general mailshot and so stand more chance of ending up in the bin.

When you follow the letter up, follow the principles outlined in the next section on making an initial telephone call.

Sample initial contact letter

SUPACOMPUTA LIMITED
Supacomputa House
Technology Business Park, Bigtown, AB1 2CD

1st April 2XXX

Dr. J. Smith
Operations Director
The Snoozeawhile Bed Company Limited
Featherbed Lane
Sleepyville
SN0 0ZE

Dear Dr. Smith

I would like to take this opportunity to introduce myself and my company to you.

Supacomputa Limited are the leading suppliers of Production Planning systems to the manufacturing industry. On average, our customers have found that our systems can save them 25% in production costs per annum. At this level of saving a system can pay for itself within ten months.

I believe one of our systems would offer Snoozeawhile a similar level of savings.

I would like to arrange a brief meeting to explain how such savings can be achieved and to see if something similar might be of interest to you. I will give you a call next week to agree a suitable time.

I look forward to meeting in the near future.

Yours sincerely

Shaun Sheppard
Sales Manager
Supacomputa Limited

If you are going to use the phone to make your initial contact, many of the same principles apply, but, because the phone enables direct dialogue with your prospect, your voice and personality will also come into play. Here are some tips for making an effective first contact phone call:

1. Make sure you know why you are making the call, what you are trying to say and what outcome you are hoping to achieve. Don't over complicate things.
2. Practise delivering your message so that you are relaxed and confident when calling.
3. Be warm and enthusiastic. A genuine belief in your product and its relevance to your prospect will quickly transmit itself, even over the phone.
4. Be concise and to the point. Don't allow the conversation to wander off track, unless you are developing a strong rapport with the prospect. Remember you are trying to get an appointment first and foremost.
5. Tell the prospect why you want a meeting, its purpose and what he will get out of it; something that will grab his attention and encourage him to agree to the meeting. Do not make any statements you cannot justify.
6. Agree a suitable time for the meeting and exactly how long it should last.
7. Do not use any jargon or acronyms. Humour may be appropriate in some circumstances, but remember you don't know the prospect, so you have no idea how he will react. Do not lapse into informality – this is an important business call.
8. Use the right names and titles. Until I have met the prospect I still like to retain the formality of using their title in the initial conversation – Dr. Smith or Miss Jones, rather than John or Jenny.
9. Confirm the meeting in writing, either by letter, fax or e-mail.

Understanding what the customer wants

Once you have secured an appointment with a prospect, the hard work (and the most enjoyable!) really starts. Seeing people face to face is the basis of just about all selling (apart from telesales) and, because people buy from people, this is where the process begins. Understanding what people want is all about questioning and listening. You might think this is common sense and therefore easy. In my experience, although it is common sense, most sales people find it very far from easy. I have been on sales calls where the sales person has almost interrogated the poor prospect into submission and still not listened to what he was being told. Sales trainers put a lot of emphasis on questioning ability, and it is important, but, if you don't listen to what you are being told – and check back with the prospect that you have actually understood – you will never get a full picture of what the prospect wants.

The prospect has agreed to see you because something in your letter or telephone call aroused his interest. You need to know exactly what it was and why. Without this information you cannot sell effectively and any attempt to do so may well lose you an order. If you burst into the prospect's office and launch into some set sales spiel, he will immediately feel that you are uninterested in him or his problems and he will wrap the meeting up very quickly. Think how you feel if some overly pushy or insensitive sales person tries to 'smoothtalk' you with some glib patter, without having the courtesy to find out what you want or even if you are interested. Your prospect will feel the same. He has agreed to see you because there is a chance you might have something to offer him. He isn't sure and he wants to find out. He is prepared to give you some of his valuable time and, if you help him, he will tell you something of his requirements. You may have to ask further questions for clarification and to gain additional information to see if it is a live sales opportunity – is there a budget? Are you talking to the decision-maker? Who else is he talking to? But the meeting will be a two-way process, and, if conducted properly, an exchange of information that satisfies both parties.

Reconfirm how much time he can spend with you. Do not exceed it unless he agrees, and tailor your approach accordingly. Not only is this professional, it tells the prospect that you value his time and appreciate the fact that he is spending some of it with you. Reconfirm what you both hope to get out the meeting. By setting the meeting up professionally, a proper dialogue can take place because both parties know what to expect. Take notes – ask permission if necessary – because you will never remember everything after the meeting and who knows what details might be important. Listen as much to what is not said as is said and observe his body language – you can pick up a lot of information this way. For example, if the prospect sits back in his seat, very relaxed and gives a fluid, off the cuff résumé of the situation, it's a fair bet he has given such a review several times before. You then need to find out if it was to your competitors or whether the requirement is so pressing it is a constant topic of discussion within the prospect's company. Whatever you do, do not interrupt when the prospect is talking and give him your whole attention.

Presenting your solution
The whole purpose of this initial meeting has been to sell something. Either you will be able to close the prospect for an order, or, if the solution is larger or more complex, you will be closing him on a decision to move to the next stage. The only way you can get such a decision is to demonstrate that your product or service solves his problems. If you have questioned and listened effectively, presenting your solution will be all the easier. You will know what the customer needs, as well as the things he would like, and you will be able to tailor your presentation to ensure that your offering covers these in detail.

You will also know why he agreed to see you and what sort of opportunity you are faced with. In addition, during the course of your discussions, you will have started to get some idea of what sort of person you are dealing with – whether he is 'open' or 'closed,' warm or cold – and you can adjust your approach accordingly. In presenting your solution you are seeking to persuade the prospect of your offering's suitability. You are trying to build up an image in the prospect's mind that positions your product or service as the natural choice.

The basic steps of a good presentation include:

1.   Always keep your message simple and check that your prospect understands what you are telling him at regular intervals. Maintain a clear and logical flow to your presentation. Summarise key points and ask if there is anything unclear or problematic in order to unearth objections or queries.

2.   Whenever you can, demonstrate what you are saying. Use your sales presenter, a PC presentation, brochures, a white board, even pieces of paper if necessary. If the customer can visualise what you have been telling him, he will understand it better. If you have samples, make sure you demonstrate them clearly and efficiently.

3.   Avoid the use of jargon, technical phrases or marketing-speak. Explain them if they are unavoidable. For example, you might know that ERP stands for Enterprise Resource Planning or that CRM stands for Customer Relationship Management, but your prospect might not. Even if he does, he might not really know what they are. Your prospect might even look as if he understands even if he doesn't and he may not want to ask because he feels he ought to know and can't say anything through embarrassment. Such concerns will distract your prospect and affect the amount of information he can take in. This can have a very real bearing on how effective your

presentation is. All industries and markets have jargon and we have all become immersed in marketing-speak, to the point where it becomes second nature. Encourage your prospect to stop you at any time if anything is unclear or if he needs an explanation.

4.   Sell benefits, not features; solutions not products or services. In presenting your offerings, it is important to remember that all the bells and whistles in the world – the features of your offering, if you like – will not sell anything unless they provide a specific benefit to your prospect. He is less interested in what your product consists of than in what it can do for him. He is looking for a solution to his problems. For example, if you are looking for a new car and have told the sales person that safety is a key issue for you, you will not want to hear that his car has a 3.0 litre engine and can do 0-62 kph in five seconds. The sales person will need to emphasise the fact that a large and powerful engine is invaluable for overtaking safely and for helping to accelerate out of dangerous circumstances, as well as providing a relaxed cruising ability. The feature is a large and powerful engine – the benefit needs to be tailored to suit the prospect's individual requirement. In this case, safety rather than performance.

5.   Having taken the time to understand what your prospect is looking for, your presentation will need to be adjusted accordingly. Just launching into a set spiel will get you nowhere and will make your prospect feel that the previous twenty minutes' questioning was a waste of time. Naturally, you will want to emphasise your strengths and minimise your weaknesses, concentrate on anything unique which differentiates you from the competition, and demonstrate what benefits can be gained from your solution. But you cannot afford for him to think, ''So what?'' when you reveal your company's

'killer' selling point. The prospect is unique and must be treated as such. Adjusting your presentation so that it is aligned with his specific requirements is a prerequisite. Otherwise he will become disinterested as he struggles to see what is in it for him.

6. Never exaggerate your claims or the abilities of your offering and always provide proof to back up your message. References, press articles, testimonials, technical information, analyst's reports or research data can all be very powerful sales tools. If other customers are happy to endorse your solution, or if you have independent evidence to prove, for example, how it can save the prospect money, there is much less chance of him doubting your claims.

7. If the customer queries anything and you do not have an answer, don't be tempted to make it up. Admit that you need to find out and then do so, getting back to the prospect as quickly as possible. If you need an order number and a signature to complete a contract, makes sure your prospect knows in advance rather than surprising him at the last minute.

8. Quote prices with authority and do not be tempted to rush in with discounts or special offers. Save these for the negotiations. Be open about contractual terms and conditions and make sure the customer is clear about the terms of engagement, i.e. what he will have to do if he wants to order. If the customer has indicated that price will be an issue, emphasise value for money, return on investment, the benefits and advantages, rather than the cost. Many sales people fall down at this point, either through worry or laziness, yet this is the topic the customer is most interested in. He wants to know whether he can afford all the nice things you have told him about and he wants to know how he can acquire them. Be open, honest and professional – you have nothing to hide or apologise for.

9. Be aware of the prospect at all times – keep listening carefully and observe body language. It is possible when presenting to get wrapped up in the message you are delivering and so miss out on the prospect's behaviour. Enquiries about price, colour, style, delivery times, contractual terms and so on are all potential buying signals. Sitting rigid with arms folded, drumming on the table, or staring out of the window while fiddling with a pen would tend to indicate that the prospect is not as excited by what you are saying as you would like. Also, in full flow, you can be tempted to ignore a customer's need to ask questions. If he has a burning need to ask something and you ignore it, not only does he become concerned that you don't have an answer; the need to ask the question stops him from taking in any further information.

10. Traditionally, sales people have been told never to knock the competition if they want to appear professional. I would not disagree with this in general, but would add – why mention the competition at all? Unless the prospect asks about them specifically, why raise the possibility of alternatives?

11. Always support your company, its policies and procedures and don't be tempted to knock any aspect of its products and services. This will only undermine the positive message you are delivering.

12. Be enthusiastic. Enthusiasm is infectious and if you believe in what you are selling, your prospect will be encouraged to be receptive, if not immediately convinced. Enthusiasm is the main reason why needs are converted into desires. Once stimulated, the fear of losing out if he does not order immediately, or the desire to get something ahead of anyone else, will make your prospect much more keen to order. Don't, however, force the issue. There is nothing as irritating as false good humour.

The proposal or quotation

At some point in the proceedings you will have to give the customer a price for your offering. Many sales people are afraid of this and worry that, no matter how cheap the price, the customer will automatically say it is too expensive. In many cases they are right! The customer will nearly always query the price, but that doesn't mean you should be afraid of quoting one, or of discussing pricing openly during the sales process. The customer will not buy anything until he knows how much it costs and, if he queries the price and starts trying to negotiate, it is a good sign that he is keen to buy.

Depending on the type and nature of your solution, the way you present your price will vary. Perhaps you have a published price list and can quote a price directly, or perhaps your offering is complex and you have to prepare a written quotation. In many cases, especially in formal tendering situations or where the solution is highly technical, you will need to produce a written proposal to support the quotation. However you deliver your price, remember that it is legally binding and needs to be delivered professionally. If terms and conditions are involved, always ensure the customer is aware of them and understands them. Never be tempted to cut corners when quoting. Make sure you include any extras that might be required to provide a total solution and, if you have to deliver a supporting proposal, ensure that you do so as professionally as possible.

Some companies employ Bid Managers or Technical Support staff to help prepare proposals and tenders, but don't forget that a proposal is first and foremost a sales document. It may well be true that the customer will tend to look at the price first, but, if you have not answered all of his questions or fail to reinforce the key messages of your sales campaign, the effort involved in producing the document may well be wasted. Producing proposals can be very time-consuming and some-times costly – I have seen timescales of many months and budgets of up to £1 million allocated to the answering of some tenders – but it is essential that the sales person keeps involved in the process. He may not be able to answer detailed technical questions or complex contractual requirements, but his input in how the document looks and what sort of overall message is delivered is essential. Any proposal or quotation is a key part of the sales process and is, as such, the sales person's responsibility. These are an essential tool for furthering a sale and need to be handled professionally and with confidence.

Forecasting and pipeline development

Forecasting is an important part of the sales process. Most sales people hate doing it and very few companies train people in forecasting, but it is an essential procedure for three key reasons:

1. It gives the company a good idea of what sort of business to expect in the short, medium and long term. Decisions about production schedules, product offerings, staffing levels, investment, advertising and marketing strategies, and so on, are all based on what sort of business might be coming along in the future. The more accurate the forecast, the better such planning can be – and the better the service the company can provide to its sales force in return.

2. It gives the sales person and his management an idea of how his effort is being converted into sales and gives everyone an idea of whether he will achieve his targets or not. It helps to pinpoint which products and services and which types of customers are producing the best results so that effort can be channelled accordingly. It also gives an idea of where peaks and troughs are developing and what action needs to be taken to help the company hit its monthly, quarterly and yearly goals. A forecast can also show if a sales person is concentrating on just a few products or customers and whether he needs additional training or support to widen his capabilities.

3.   It provides a competitive focus for the sales force and an incentive to try and do better than their colleagues. Such competition is healthy and can help drive a sales team to greater success. Discussing the forecast openly at sales meetings can also be a source of good ideas and a valuable exchange of information.

Many sales people fear forecasting because they don't want to expose their hand or give away what they are (or are not!) doing if they can help it. Yet forecasting is a valuable tool for the sales person as well as for his company. It is certainly something he will be unable to avoid and the better he is at providing accurate and timely information, the more he will be appreciated.

Forecasting is the process of estimating what business is likely to be won in the future. It includes estimates of the value of that business and a date when the order will be taken. There are all sorts of systems, of varying degrees of complexity, and each company will have its own approach. The main aim is to be as accurate as possible and, although it can never be an exact science, the very best sales people forecast with great consistency. The also-rans don't. A basic forecast might look like the following simple example and will contain information on the company who might place the order, how big the order might be and a date by when the order will be closed.

Getting the order value and the closing date right is very important and many companies measure their sales people on accuracy. A forecast might also contain a probability of the business happening at all. Such probabilities can be quite complicated and each company will have its own guidelines, but the aim is to try and indicate the likelihood of a piece of business happening within the indicated timescale, if at all. Once such probability is allocated, it is possible to factor the order value by that probability and this is often seen as a much more accurate measure of the actual business that will be closed. Typically a sales person should be forecasting at least three to four times his annual target on the basis that he will only win between one in three or one in four of the opportunities he is chasing.

Sample Forecast

Company	Order Value	Closing Date	Probability	Factored Value
ABC Ltd	£ 150,000.00	15/01/XX	0.1	£ 15,000.00
Snoozeawhile Ltd	£ 500,000.00	25/01/XX	0.5	£ 250,000.00
Perkins plc	£ 225,000.00	27/02/XX	0.2	£ 45,000.00
Jenkins Tools	£ 100,000.00	03/03/XX	0.8	£ 80,000.00
Britelite Ltd	£ 750,000.00	13/03/XX	0.5	£ 375,000.00
Cabinetco	£ 250,000.00	20/05/XX	0.2	£ 50,000.00
Wemake Tools	£ 100,000.00	16/06/XX	0.1	£ 10,000.00
Bestbeds Inc	£ 500,000.00	20/08/XX	0.1	£ 50,000.00
Jones and Son	£ 100,000.00	25/10/XX	0.5	£ 50,000.00
Tinkers Best Ltd	£ 650,000.00	10/11/XX	0.2	£ 130,000.00
Totals	**£3,325,000.00**			**£1,055,000.00**
Annual Target	**£1,000,000.00**			
Sold year to date	£ 50,000.00			

A sales person's forecast is based directly on his pipeline. From his prospecting activity, he will have identified a number of potential sales opportunities from the leads he has generated, often called Suspects and Prospects, and these form a pipeline of potential business. In reality a pipeline is not a static process, but a dynamic one, with new leads generating suspects and prospects on a continual basis to take the place of orders that are closed or lost. Typically, a Suspect is a lead which has been canvassed sufficiently to confirm the likelihood of business, but not qualified enough to confirm the exact nature of that business (size, timescale etc.). A forecast is normally made up of Prospects, but rarely Suspects, because only business which is well qualified and accurately assessed can be forecasted with any degree of confidence.

Simple pipeline

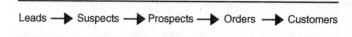

Leads ➤ Suspects ➤ Prospects ➤ Orders ➤ Customers

Keeping records

Most sales people dislike bureaucracy and paperwork, but keeping a simple record of all of your prospects, suspects and customers is essential. Knowledge and contacts are some of the most valuable assets a sales person owns. By keeping a note, not just of the company's name, address and telephone number, but of personal contact details – secretaries' names, family details if appropriate, mobile phone numbers, personal extension numbers and e-mail addresses, products sold, procurement cycles and procedures, company structure, sign off authorities and even some thoughts on the 'political' structure – a sales person can provide a much more personalised and individual service, as well as being 'on the ball' should he need to move quickly in a sales situation. Keeping such information up-to-date can seem a bit arduous at times, but professionals have always done this and, with today's computer systems shouldering a lot of the burden, no sales person should be short of accurate customer information.

A professional sales person should also have a good idea of his productivity – the number of appointments he makes with customers, how many quotations these generate and how many orders he closes from those quotations. Such statistics are a very good indicator of his effectiveness. They can also be useful if his sales manager is worried about work rate and productivity. It depends very much on which market they are working in, but it is very easy to measure a sales person's strike rate (the ratio of bids or quotations issued to the number of orders received). In the computer industry, they typically close between 1:3 to 1:4 orders they are chasing, but it can often take many meetings, calls and quotations to get into a closing position. Anything that helps to make the process more effective will close more business and knowing how good you currently are is the first step in improving things. Just guessing is not good enough.

Some companies expect sales people to keep weekly call plans and to fill out daily call reports. Many 'professionals' see this is as an imposition and look on it as something 'juniors' do. I suggest that a real professional might want to keep some sort of record of where he is spending his time, and how well he is converting it into orders, because it will make him more effective and will help him pinpoint any area where he might need training or assistance. Also, if you only have a limited number of customers, planning your time so that they do not become fed up with you is important and a record of whom you have seen and when becomes even more important.

Delivering and managing the relationship

Once you have closed a piece of business with a prospect, he becomes a customer. The relationship you developed in order to win that first piece of business will have to mature and evolve in order to accommodate the bedding in of your first order, as well as the possibility of gaining additional business. There are three points to consider:

1. Having sold him an initial offering, can you sell him more, for example, add-ons and future upgrades, or will he need something else from your product portfolio?
2. Are there other departments, divisions or parts of the Group which might need your products and services? Can you use your first sale to the company to any

advantage in helping leverage business elsewhere?

3. What are the competition doing, and where, and how can you protect your position?

The traditional approach in selling has always been to sell high and wide – to make contact with the organisation at the highest possible level, e.g. the directors, and to talk to the widest number of people. This principle holds true for account management. Getting to know as many people as you can at your account will help you to sell more and will help to minimise any contact that the competition might be attempting to make. It goes without saying that you must ensure all pre- and post-sales work is conducted to the highest possible standard and that anyone from your own company who works on the account should uphold your own high standards of service. Do not restrict yourself to the department or division in which you made your first sale. Canvass as many departments as you can and, if possible, use your existing customers as 'internal' sales people – to spread the word that you are worth talking to. Do not forget that, if the company you are dealing with is part of a group, your products and services may be applicable elsewhere, even if another sales person might cover the specific territory. Make sure you pass on the leads. The more your company sells to them as a whole, the stronger your own position will become.

The key to success in account management is to make yourself indispensable (without ignoring your other customers and the rest of your territory) and to know your client's business thoroughly – buying cycles, political and organisational structure, purchasing procedures, as well as their plans for the future. The more you know about them, and the more they come to trust and rely on you, the more able you will be to influence their decision-making process. Do not allow yourself to become stale or complacent. The competition will always be on the lookout for a way back in and any sign of weakness on your behalf will be exploited ruthlessly. The stronger the relationship you have with your customer, the more effective the 'lockout' capability you will have with regards to the competition – but only if the service you provide continues to be outstanding.

Do not just concentrate on the here and now, but look to the future. History shows that positions of strength **always** become a weakness over time. You will never be in pole position forever, but you can sustain your leading position for a very long time if you are a source of new ideas and support your customer's business drives for the future. This is much more likely to occur if the customer trusts your judgment and looks to you for advice and guidance, but it means that you must be up-to-date and fully conversant with all new products, business opportunities and developments, as well as understanding your customer's business thoroughly.

Treating customers well is largely down to providing an excellent service, but there are additional ways of rewarding customers for continued business, for acting as reference sites or for special or outstanding orders. Overt gifts are heavily frowned upon in today's marketplace and I have even known customers refuse meals or invitations to drinks for fear of appearing overly close to a particular supplier. However, invitations to events sponsored by your company, like charitable functions or sports fixtures, can often be acceptable and many customers will be flattered if asked to provide a keynote speech at one of your own company's events or conferences. Special offers, user group privileges, loyalty discounts and bonuses, the chance to buy new products early, involvement with product development – all these, and more, are excellent ways of rewarding major customers, but never forget the personal approach. Send Christmas cards to all key customers, give company diaries and promotional items away freely (it also helps to keep your company's name in view!) and take an interest in your customers on a more personal level, congratulating them for promotion or major wins of their own.

Reference selling

Once you have sold something and the implementation has gone smoothly, the customer is happy with everything and there is the chance of repeat business, you may want to approach him to act as a reference site or to provide a testimonial of some sort. Referrals and testimonials are some of the most effective sales tools any sales person can use. After all, if a customer is prepared, independently of your own organisation, to tell the world how great your products and service are, your effort in finding new business will be seriously reduced. There is nothing so powerful as being able to say to a prospective customer, "ABC Co Ltd use our products. Here is the name of their head buyer. Why don't you give him a call to see what he thinks of our widgets?"

Obviously, this will only be any good if the head buyer at ABC Co Ltd thinks your widgets are the best thing since sliced bread! Reference selling is only possible if you have an excellent relationship with your customer. Don't abuse it. I have known some reference sites become fed up with the number of calls being made on them – after all they have a job to do and it isn't acting as unpaid sales people for your company. They are prepared to act as a reference because they like you and the product and/or service is so good they are happy to talk about it, but they do not want to be taken advantage of or exploited.

In some cases, customers know that, if the product they have bought is sold widely, then the chances of extra development, price reductions and new services will increase. But remember that, if such customers decide to band together and form a Users Group – an association of users formed to share experience and look at the ongoing development of the product – it can become a double-edged sword. Users Groups can be an excellent source of additional sales, references and development ideas, but they can also become demanding and powerful as their size increases, seeking to influence your company's products and pricing to their own advantage.

In many companies, the process of gathering references and testimonials will be handled by a different department from sales, often the Marketing or PR department. Do not allow them free access to your account until you are happy that your customer is comfortable with such an approach and you are sure they will stick to their brief. You own the relationship with your customer and it should not be abused. In many cases, the customer's senior management will need to vet and approve anything which will link their name with yours in the wider marketplace. This can be an excellent opportunity for stronger relationships to be forged at a higher level and help to gain you contact in areas previously denied to you. For example, if your customer's Managing Director needs to authorise a press release that your company wishes to produce, announcing the sale of your flagship product to his company, it makes sense (and is common courtesy) to use your own MD to make the contact and to ask for permission. Once such peer-to-peer relationships are established, a much closer bond between the customer and your own company can develop. But do not forget that you still own the relationship and need to be included in or informed of everything that takes place.

It is worth noting that some companies, although delighted with your products and services, will not wish to tell anyone else, especially if they perceive they have developed a competitive edge by using your offerings! Respect this and do not abuse confidentiality or exploit the connection if it isn't authorised. It may be very tempting to use a particular company's name in connection with your products or services if they are particularly influential in the marketplace, but if they haven't given permission, it could rebound on you later on. It goes without saying that reference customers should get the very best service your company can provide. But also remember that they are customers first and foremost and not a part of your own company. Sometimes relationships can become so close that there is a blurring of the normal lines of business. Never allow this to affect your professionalism.

3

PLANNING

What is planning?

Success in business does not happen by accident. It involves hard work and dedication. But, if that hard work is not channelled effectively or is spent in the wrong way, it will be wasted and success will be elusive. Planning helps to avoid this. It is a simple process that gives an individual or an organisation the opportunity to stand back from the mad rush of normal business life and to take stock of where they are and where they are going.. After all, if you plunge headfirst into the marketplace with no clear idea of what direction you need to take, you are unlikely to arrive at a satisfactory destination. The modern business environment leaves no room for vagueness, uncertainty or doubt and, if you do not know what it is you really want to achieve and have given no thought to how you might achieve it, you will get nowhere. By focusing on three important items – goals, timing and execution – the planning process will help you decide when you should do things and how you should go about them, in order to get what you want.

A General would never start out on a military campaign without a detailed plan of attack. He cannot afford to waste time or resources and he must maximise his chances of success. He envisages a successful outcome before he even starts the campaign and through the planning process attempts to turn that vision into reality. In the same way, if you go to your bank manager and ask him to lend you money to finance your great new idea, he will immediately ask to see your business plan. He already knows you believe it will be a success, but he needs to believe it too; which means proving to him that you know what you are doing. A business plan shows you have researched the market, looked at the competition, considered cash flow, estimated the return on investment, and planned the steps you need to take to make your idea a reality.

What does planning mean for sales people?
The sales person's primary reason for existence is to sell things. We may have a few other peripheral functions, but, if we don't sell enough to satisfy our quotas or targets, the companies we work for fail to reach their goals and we end up without a job. Anything that can give us an edge in this process, make us more effective and which helps to improve our productivity, has got to be of benefit. As professionals we are, in many ways, running our own businesses, albeit with the safety net of a larger organisation to support us. And, like a CEO (Chief Executive Officer), we need to have a clear vision of the way ahead. Success doesn't happen by accident and you can bet your bottom dollar that your competition, customers and even some of your colleagues will be developing plans to further their own aims and objectives. They won't necessarily have your best interests at heart either and their success will often be at your expense! Planning in itself cannot guarantee success because, as with any tool, it is up to you how you use it. But, without planning, success can only happen by chance – and luck is a fickle commodity at the best of times.

At the most basic level, there are only two things a sales person needs to plan for – earning a living and keeping his job. Both of these can be achieved by planning to meet the sales target. Yet, for many, planning seems like one chore too many – either an overhead that they haven't got the time to bother with, or something so menial that it is beneath them – something 'juniors' do. Many of them feel it is 'all in their heads' anyway, so why go through the effort of writing things down and setting goals and objectives; devising strategies and plans? You would be amazed by the number of 'professional' sales people who feel like this and who receive their targets at the beginning of the year with no clue as to where the business will come from. They struggled to reach their targets the previous year (if they were lucky! A significant percentage do not reach their targets and only manage to do just enough to keep their jobs) and gave no thought to preparing for the next, so they have a mountain to climb from day one. The true professional on the other hand knows where he wants to be this year, next year and the year after that. His target is basically an irrelevance because he already knows what he is doing and why; where he is going and how he will get there. His target is just one step on the way to a larger goal, and its achievement is confirmation that his wider objectives will be realised.

Planning – A personal perspective

I am not a great fan of lots of forms and reports, lists of things to do and record keeping. Filling in paperwork is definitely an overhead I can do without and I guess that most sales people feel the same way. That's why, when it comes to planning, I try to keep it as simple and easy as possible; noting everything in my diary rather than producing separate plans and charts. I make a list of the things I want to achieve (both at home and at work) and then break them down into the steps I have to take in order to get there. Each of these steps has to happen by a certain date if I am to achieve my goals in time and the diary makes this very simple to record and monitor. (Writing this book was always a long term objective, although I neglected to put a timescale to it so I shouldn't be surprised that it has taken me so long!) Writing these steps down helps to ensure that I don't forget things and that I don't keep jumping around trying to do everything at once, but completing very little. It also helps me, if I don't succeed in getting where I want to be, to pinpoint where I went wrong, which helps me to plan more effectively next time.

Another advantage of keeping a good record of what you are doing, and what you plan to do, is that you can guarantee your manager will pounce on you at some stage demanding a written report justifying your work-rate or forecast. You know he is being kicked from above for the information and only passing things along, but if you don't provide him with what he needs, he appears inefficient and so will take it out on you. If you have your finger on the pulse, know what you are doing and why, and are on top of your business, writing the report will be much easier than having to create (make-up?!) things from scratch.

Three simple steps

Planning can be as simple or as detailed as you want to make it, but to be of any value, you must use it. Therefore, planning should be easy. The aim is to create a route map to get you from where you are to where you want to be as quickly and effectively as possible. For me, the process falls naturally into three basic steps – Plan, Prioritise, Act.

1. Plan

Decide what you are going to do over the next few years and what you would like to achieve. Write these objectives down. You already know that you have this year's target to achieve, but there may be other goals that you are keen to pursue, like promotion or becoming top salesman, owning a Ferrari or setting up your own company. It doesn't matter how big or challenging these goals are, so long as you are prepared to put your heart and soul into achieving them. They must be something you want so badly that you will not be put off at the first obstacle or problem. Ideally, they should encourage you to stretch your capabilities as well. Give them an end date. The human mind has a tendency always to respond to instructions and deadlines and, by writing down your list of goals, your mind will respond automatically by trying to complete them. Review your list regularly to keep your mind on track.

In drawing up your objectives, it may help to use a simple tool (often used by Human Resources departments when setting objectives for appraisals) – SMART – to make them more realistic and focused:

Specific   Your objectives should be simple to understand and easily defined. If it helps, include a product or service, monetary value, or both.

Measurable   They should have some tangible outcome so that you can easily see whether you have achieved them or, if not, how far you got.

Achievable   They should be something that you can reason-ably expect to achieve within the timescale, although it may require effort.

Realistic   But they should be something that you and/or your company can reasonably expect to deliver.

Timed   Finally they should have a time limit otherwise they could go on for ever, e.g. I will achieve xyz within three months, or by the 1st June.

On this basis, at the very least your key goal for this year should be – 'I will achieve my yearly target of x amount of new business sales by the end of the financial year'. It is Specific in that it is easy to understand; it is Measurable in that you can easily monitor how you are doing; it is Achievable because it is something a professional sales person ought to be able to achieve; it is Realistic because the products and services your company produces will support such an achievement and it has a Timed end date which cannot be exceeded.

You then need to plan how you will go about it and the simplest approach is to break it down into a number of steps or mini-goals which, when added together, will help you to reach your main objective. Again, these steps should be written down and monitored regularly. The success of your main objective depends on each of these individual steps being completed satisfactorily and on time. By completing each step successfully, you will be encouraged that you are on the right track and will be motivated to move to the next step and then the next until your objective is achieved.

Let's look at this in a bit more detail. If your main goal is to achieve your target, you will need to plan a number of individual sales campaigns in order to get there, for example: I will sell a complete production planning system to the Snoozeawhile Bed Company, which will account for half of my yearly target, by the end of the second quarter in this financial year. In order to achieve this objective a number of individual steps will need to be taken in order to be successful (it goes without saying that you have already discovered Snoozeawhile are in the market for a new system!).

You will have to find out who the decision-maker is and what information, presentations, and demonstrations he and his team will need in order for them to be able to make a decision. This will need a number of meetings which will have to be planned and timetabled very carefully so that each one furthers your aim to secure the order. You need to know who the current supplier is and what the rest of the competition are doing so you can counteract their activities – it is important to lead rather than follow. You will probably need to draft in some resources from your own company to help with specific tasks like contract negotiations or technical presentations and you will have to make sure that these are available to you at the times you require them. A reference visit to an existing customer of yours might be appropriate and will need to be timetabled. A proposal and quotation will need to be prepared. You may even have to take account of political activity within Snoozeawhile in case your decision-maker could be influenced by his own career aspirations or an internal power struggle. You will also have to check whether your desire to close a deal within six months is matched by the prospect's ability to make a decision in the same timescale.

However, all of this could be subject to change without notice! Planning is not a fixed procedure which you do once and then forget about. It is dynamic and ongoing. As events develop you will gain new information and insights, or something unexpected will happen, which will mean your plan will have to be updated or adapted. But, because your overall objectives haven't changed, you always know where you are going and why. The individual steps within the plan may need to be modified, but the overall framework and outcome remains fixed, which enables you to channel your efforts effectively and not get side-tracked. Every meeting, every source of information, every phone call and every letter should be part of the plan. But, whatever steps you take, they should have one single purpose – to move you closer to achieving your objective. In the case of Snoozeawhile this means closing the deal so that you are one step nearer to achieving your yearly target.

2. Prioritise

As sales people, we only have a finite amount of time available to us. There are only 365 days in a year and, assuming no illness, by the time we take out holidays (say 25 days), training courses (say 10 days), internal events like sales meetings, appraisals and so on (say 2 days a month – 24 days) and weekends (104 days), we are left with something like 200 or so working days in which to achieve our objectives. This is not very long when you consider how much needs to be done, yet some sales people use the time to overachieve and many don't. What is the difference?

Time Management is a concept most people are familiar with. It is all about common sense – about fitting all the things we have to do into the time available to us. The professional sales person should already have a pretty good idea of what he has to do on any given day. Having broken his objectives down into keys steps and made a note of when they need to be done, his diary is likely to be fairly full most days. He won't be scratching around for things to do. But there is one task he needs to carry out before he starts on his list – he needs to prioritise what he has to do in order to make the most effective use of his time. This is best done just before you leave work in the evening so that you don't get up the following morning wondering what the day has in store for you. Your mind can be preparing to get started even before you get to work and, since most people are at their most productive in the morning, you can use your most productive time to greatest effect.

There is a saying, ''Don't do with great energy that which does not need to be done'', but it is a sad fact that many people do this all the time, kidding themselves they are busy when they are, in reality, achieving very little at all. The key to success is making sure that you spend your most productive time on those things which help you to achieve your objectives. And, in your case this means selling. Getting that proposal out, generating a quotation, making sure production can deliver on time, or ensuring that billing include the right discounts are all important – perhaps critical to the success of a particular opportunity – but communication with customers is the most important. Everything else can be slotted in behind.

In prioritising your time, remember that at best you only have about nine to ten hours to play with on any given day. Of course you can stay late, skip lunch or get in early, but too much of that will cost you dearly. You must allocate time for relaxation, exercise, hobbies and, most importantly, for your family. What is the point in earning the commission if you can't enjoy spending some of it? And don't forget to eat properly. I know many sales people who neglect mealtimes. They cite pressures of work and lack of time and then wonder why their energy levels tail off. They feel tired and drained and are often completely unproductive by late afternoon.

On the other hand, don't hang around the coffee machine chatting, take long lunch breaks or allow other people to waste your time. You are at work for a reason – to earn a living – and you can only do that if you sell things. Once you have prioritised everything you have to do, you won't have any spare time left over. I'll say that again – **you won't have any spare time left over**. Every minute of your day at work should be accounted for and should, in some measure, help to advance your objectives. If you complete everything on your list, prospecting for new business should be a priority.

3. Act

The planning process is just a tool. It can help you sort out what you should be doing and when, but it can't act for you. Only you can do that. And only action can make things happen. Action is all about completing tasks, so, once you have got your list in priority order, get on and do the first thing on the list. Don't get side-tracked or prevaricate. When it is completed, do the second thing and then the third, and so on. If you are unable to complete a task because you are waiting for someone else to provide information or finish something off, make everyone involved aware of the situation and then put the task to one side until it can be rescheduled and forget about it. Don't worry or become preoccupied. Get on with the next thing on your list. Some days you may not complete everything, but you will have completed the most important things, which will give you a sense of achievement and move you closer to your key objectives. At the end of the day, review what you have achieved and, if anything was not completed, consider if it really needs to be done at all. If so, prioritise it along with the next day's tasks. Do not be a slave to your list or allow it to restrict you in any way. It is just a tool for making the best use of your time and, if something really important crops up, you will find the time to deal with it.

Protracted timescales
In large, complex sales opportunities it may take many months (sometimes years) to close the deal and this presents a number of problems for the sales person involved:

1. He needs to keep himself and his team motivated.
2. He needs to demonstrate to his management that he is working towards a resolution, even if things appear to be moving very slowly.
3. He needs to be managing his customers and pushing them to make decisions and move things forward to his agenda rather than the competition's.

This is where planning comes into its own. Your overall objective is to win the deal, but (let us say it will take 12 months to close) monitoring progress and ensuring you have control of the sales process will only happen if you break it down into manageable chunks and mini-objectives. This means that every month (every week if necessary), you will have goals to aim for and certain key objectives to reach. You and your team will be motivated to achieve them and, in so doing, your management will be able to see that progress is being maintained. Your customers will also welcome the fact that you provide information on time, assist them in keeping to the timetable and make the decision-making process as easy as possible. They are just as concerned about protracted timescales as you are. They have a problem that needs resolving and, although they need to take time making the decision, they cannot afford for things to drag on too long. If you are professional in managing the situation, and are clear about exactly what you are doing and what needs to be done – keeping everyone informed and regularly reviewing the situation – a successful outcome is much more likely and progress can more easily be monitored.

What to go for and what not
When planning, you will have to make some decisions about which sales opportunities you will chase and which you will not bother with. This process is sometimes called the bid/no bid decision, or qualifying in or out of an opportunity, and it is an increasingly important skill for sales people to learn. Desperate or inexperienced sales people might be tempted to try and go for every single opportunity they can find, regardless of their chance of winning, but this is a sure fire way to waste time and energy.

Professional sales people will have researched their territories to the point that they know where the most promising business will come from. They know their efforts are best spent on opportunities they can win and on customers or prospects who are most receptive to their sales message. When prospecting they try to search for those companies who most closely fit this profile. It doesn't mean they reject everything else, but it does mean that they will look at each opportunity very carefully and only bid for those where they have a realistic chance of success. Sometimes it is worth bidding for things that you will not win but where the cost of bidding is low and the information you gain is high and will help you win significant business in the future. However, such an approach is a luxury and should only be considered after consultation with your company's management.

Deciding what to bid for or not can be very complex, depending on how water-tight you want to make it, and there are dozens of formalised ways of going about the process. I have even worked for companies where the whole bid/no bid process became a bureaucratic hurdle that deliberately rejected all but the most meticulously planned and justified opportunities in an attempt to improve their strike rate and to ensure that limited resources could be allocated effectively. To a certain extent they were successful, but the cost in management time and the turn-over in disgruntled sales people, who failed to get bids through, was very high. There was also the problem of how far the policy should be taken: an improvement in the strike rate from 5:1 to 3:1 is probably worth the effort, but getting it down to 2:1 might not be. It is also worth bearing in mind that any such process is only as good as the information available to you and can never be 100% accurate.

For me, the bid/no bid process should be as simple and as unbureaucratic as possible. It is the sales person's responsibility to justify and plan his time as it is his target and objectives he is trying to reach. He may choose to discuss certain opportunities with his manager – and his manager will certainly want to discuss things with him if his strike rate is poor – but if he can't justify to himself why he is chasing a particular opportunity then he is, frankly, wasting his time. The most effective way I have found to manage the process – one that doesn't involve an excessive amount of time and effort – is a simple tool that one of my sales managers introduced me to at the beginning of my sales career – SCOTSMAN.

Solution   Does your solution meet all or the majority of your prospect's requirements? Can it be made to fit with some realistic modifications?

Competition   Who are the competition? Are the competition better placed than you? Does the prospect favour them? Has the prospect heard of your company at all? How many companies will be allowed to bid for the business? What selection criteria will be used?

Only me   Does your company, product or service have any unique selling points that no-one else can claim? Can you capitalise on them?

Timescales   What timescales is the prospect working to and can you accommodate them? Are they realistic? What is their procurement cycle?

Strategy   Have you drawn up a plan of action for this opportunity? Do you know what steps you will take and what information you need to help ensure a successful outcome?

Money   Does the prospect have a budget and is it realistic? Can he afford your products and services? When will the money be signed off? Is the money likely to be hijacked for a more critical project?

Authority   Are you talking to the person who has the authority to place the order and spend the budget? What is the company structure and who reports to whom? Are there any people who can influence the decision-maker? Have you seen them all?

Need   Does your prospect really have a need that will be satisfied by your product or service or is he just looking for information? Has he developed a business case to justify such a purchase? Is he acting alone? If he needs authorisation, does he have the support of senior management?

Go through this process with all of your prospects and opportunities. If you don't know the answers or have negatives against a number of headings, consider what is involved in getting more information or in turning those negatives into positives. If you are unable to gain further information or the effort involved in turning things around is considerable, you should seriously question whether this is an opportunity you should be pursuing. Obviously, the tool is only any good if you are completely honest with yourself when answering the questions, but who are you kidding if you fudge things?

Customers also tend to appreciate this approach. They don't want their time wasted evaluating bids which don't fulfil their requirements and, if you are clear about what you can and can't deliver, you will build up a degree of trust and respect. That doesn't mean that, in certain circumstances, you shouldn't try and help them change their minds. That's what selling is all about and, if they are going down a certain path because they are unaware that a better one exists, they should be encouraged to look again. But be realistic if you take this approach and don't waste your efforts if a particular prospect is hell-bent on something you can't supply and won't consider anything else at all.

Planning your territory

Most sales people have a patch, territory or customer list from which they have to generate their yearly target. These can often be a major bone of contention, especially if you view everyone else's territory as potentially more lucrative than your own. The patch you inherit may well have been poorly managed by a previous salesman. It may even be considered a 'desert' with no business potential and insufficient existing customers to enable you to hit your target. Yet, complaining about your sales territory will earn you a reputation you probably don't want – and it will waste time and energy which you should be devoting to the development of your customer base. Just because a territory has historically been bad for your company does not mean that it will always be like that. People move on, new products and services are developed, new companies move in, the competition go bust or become less competitive. Inevitably, because a patch is seen as 'bad' no-one else will have made an effort to cultivate it. Who knows what rich pickings there might be? The least you can do is go and look.

The patch you inherit may even be considered a 'desert' with no business potential.

If you inherit a very rich territory you inherit a different set of problems. The patch has been so successful in the past that your company will expect it to continue producing at the same high level for ever. This might be unrealistic, but the new sales person has the problem of managing the situation. In a very good patch he must always be on the look out for competitive action seeking to undermine existing accounts. He must continually introduce new products and services to existing customers to ensure that they keep on buying from his company. He must develop good relationships with new decision-makers at existing customers to ensure they don't defect to other suppliers. He must not allow himself to get sucked into a 'comfort zone' where he just goes around taking orders from existing customers. He must continue prospecting for new business – not just in case things turn sour at existing customers, but because he will inevitably be expected to overachieve with such a good patch and will need a steady inflow of new business to satisfy this demand.

When you assume ownership of your territory, you take full responsibility for learning everything about the customers and potential prospects in it and determining which ones are the likeliest to benefit from what you have to offer. Such a territory needs to be managed professionally to ensure that:

1. All existing customers receive sufficient post sales service to ensure that they become repeat customers and do not defect to the opposition.
2. All potential customers are encouraged to become actual customers.
3. All those who are not currently in buying mode, but who may be in the future, are kept aware of your products and services.
4. Any organisation which is never likely to be a purchaser of your products and services is identified.
5. Competitor activity is monitored.
6. Changes in the marketplace or industry are noted and addressed, which might include identifying new product areas for your company to move into.
7. New companies opening up in your patch are canvassed early.
8. You must never stop prospecting.

Keeping a balance between these requirements is often difficult, especially if one customer needs a lot of attention or a particular sales campaign becomes protracted or time-consuming. Yet there is a need to circulate around your territory in order to keep up-to-date with what is going on. Pay attention that you do not spend too much time with your best customers. They will need excellent service but, if you spend too much of your time on them, you will miss out on new opportunities elsewhere. Remember to use all of the facilities at your disposal – mail shots, faxes, letters, seminars, e-mails, telephone calls, exhibitions, telesales, company website – to keep your territory aware of you and your company. For many customers, a visit by a good professional sales person, who is up-to-date with product and market knowledge, can be an event to look forward to. He is a valuable source of information and buying from him can bring a number of additional benefits over and above a good product or price. Make sure that you provide a total service to all of your customers, large and small, so that you become indispensable.

If you have a physically large territory do not dissipate your energy by charging here, there and everywhere trying to cover a few key customers and prospects. If you have to visit a customer in a location where there are no other customers or prospects, do some prospecting in the area instead. Cold call a few companies and get the names of the buyer or decision-maker and then follow them up later on to make an appointment when you are next in that area. Don't expect to see them on the initial cold-call, but do leave a business card. Never forget to ask your existing customers if they know of anyone else who might be worth your while calling on. Do not underestimate the value of local sources of information – libraries, chambers of commerce, trade associations, the trade press – which could help to pinpoint likely prospects.

In planning your territory, do not take anything for granted. If your patch is just one customer (it happens) make sure you canvass every single department to see if there is a sales opportunity outside of your normal channels. If you have a geographic patch, make sure you take different routes back to the office to find out as much as you can about the territory. (I once found a company who became a major customer by doing this. I had no idea they existed until I took a different road and stumbled upon them by chance.) Keep in mind that travelling is not selling. It may be a necessary evil if you have a large patch or your customers are a long way away, but aim to reduce its effects on your selling time, which means planning your calling schedules accordingly.

Planning a territory – a personal perspective

Some time ago I worked for a computer company which specialised in sales to local government. As the 'rookie', I drew the short straw and got the patch which included all the very large Metropolitan Borough Councils. My company was particularly successful at selling solutions to the smaller district councils, but their success in the larger authorities was conspicuous by its absence. ICL, IBM and Bull were the main players. Consequently, no one wanted my patch and it had been poorly managed for a long time. I inherited two existing customers with small, problematic installations and no live prospects at all. My colleagues laid bets as to how long I would last. Yet, over a four year period I secured enough business to be promoted twice and to achieve President's Club twice. I made two separate plans:

1. Go and see every authority on my 'patch' and talk to the IT Directors, Departmental Heads and Directors of Finance. I made a point of keeping in touch regularly, personally and by letter, and inviting them to all relevant exhibitions and seminars. I also sent out mailshots and flyers whenever we had a major success story to tell or when a new product or service was launched. I realised that any sale I might make would be a departmental system, rather than a complete mainframe replacement, but, as some of the individual departments were bigger than whole district authorities, there was a chance I could secure some big orders. My plan was to emphasise ease of use and quality of service rather than fight the mainframe suppliers over technology. I made a point of concentrating on those departments which appeared to be getting a raw deal as central government introduced more and more changes to local legislation. It was hard work and initially unrewarding, but persistence paid off and I eventually secured two substantial orders which I was then able to develop and upgrade over time.

2. Take ownership of the two problematic installations and undertake, personally, to sort out the problems. Each was completely different, one taking three years to resolve and the other just twelve months, but my approach to them was similar – visibility. I realised that these two authorities had purchased solutions from my company for a reason and that, problems aside, those reasons were still valid. If I could re-emphasise the values that had made them choose us in the first place, while openly addressing the problems, I stood a chance of stabilising things, if not making a further sale. My predecessors had run away from the problems in the past, which had infuriated the customers, and my first meetings were extremely uncomfortable. But, as I demonstrated a degree of stamina and understanding they were not expecting, and represented their views back into my own company in such a way that we did resolve the problems, I gained a degree of respect and trust that was ultimately rewarded by significant additional business.

4

RESOURCES

What are resources?
Anything a sales person can use to help him close business more successfully could be termed a resource. Resources include a sales person's own skills and knowledge, actual physical assets like telephones or the Internet, and even other people. Today, we have more resources available to us than at any other time in history – more sources of information, more tools to increase productivity and more methods of getting a message across – and the very best sales people exploit all of these to their advantage. Unfortunately, the one resource we could all do with more of is strictly limited. Time is finite and anything that allows a sales person to maximise the effectiveness of the time available to him will improve his chances of success.

Sales people need to be familiar with, and comfortable with using, all the tools and facilities they have at their disposal, but it is a sad fact that many are not. For example: used properly, the telephone is an excellent resource for finding out information, getting a message across quickly and succinctly, and furthering relationships with customers, colleagues and prospects. Used poorly, the telephone can be a time waster and an actual barrier to success. We all take the telephone for granted and use it unconsciously – to the point where many people forget it is a business tool rather than a social resource. I'm sure you never squander your time at work by phoning your family/ bookmaker/travel agent/stockbroker, but many sales people do!

Sales people need to use a wide range of physical resources daily, in order to do their jobs properly. From letters and business cards, proposals and brochures, through sales presenters or presentation equipment, to contracts and price lists, these are just some of the tools of the trade. They may not close a deal for you, but a failure to use them effectively will almost certainly lose you business. They are essential to the smooth running of meetings, even whole sales campaigns, and can add weight to your arguments by underlining the quality and depth of the service you can provide. They help to give an image of the sort of company you work for and help to develop trust and respect in your ability to recommend a solution. It is inevitable that, if they are handled poorly, that image and trust may be damaged.

Coupled with these physical assets are the more intangible resources like information, knowledge and contacts. Information is the sales person's 'stock-in-trade' and, today, there is absolutely no excuse for anyone in business to say "I didn't know that" or "My knowledge is out of date". There are so many sources of information available that keeping abreast of what is going on is more a case of sorting out the relevant from the irrelevant, rather than finding things out from scratch. Marketing reports, surveys, directories, journals, the Internet, newspapers, colleagues, customers – useful information can come from anywhere. The successful sales person must be like a sponge, absorbing information on an ongoing basis so that he can maintain an accurate picture of the world in which he is operating.

Personal resources
Every sales person brings a complex array of personal attributes and assets to bear on his sales campaigns. Even the novice has a lot to draw on.

1. Personality

Your personality is your most fundamental resource. It determines how you present yourself to others, how you handle problems and setbacks, whether you can be trusted or not, and your whole attitude to selling. Confidence, optimism, enjoyment and enthusiasm are all determined by what sort of person you are and that will determine how successful you will be.

Your personality is one resource that, while it can be used to your advantage, cannot really be changed. I know there are lots of books available about 'improving yourself' and I accept it is possible to maximise your good points and diminish the bad to a certain extent, but 'how you are is largely how you is' and any attempt to restrict, change or 'improve' your personality will only result in falseness and insincerity. The best sales people are very comfortable with who they are and this comes across to their customers who, in turn, feel comfortable with them too.

2. Skills

Your formal education will be supported by experience and specific training and your business acumen, general knowledge and IQ will be honed and enhanced by constant use and practice. All of these will be of use to you in business and, while classroom training and book learning are no substitute for experience and natural flair, they are still vitally important in helping to develop your abilities.

3. Knowledge

A professional sales person should develop and keep up to date the following: general knowledge, business knowledge, specific market knowledge, company knowledge, and product or service knowledge. You need a detailed and thorough understanding of the wider business environment in which you work, as well as the specific demands of your own particular marketplace, in order to position your products and services effectively. You need to know what is happening globally so that you understand the framework in which all businesses work. You need to know your own market sector intimately, especially competitors, the impact of new technology, who is who and what companies are involved. You need to know your own company and products inside out so that you can answer questions easily and in detail – it can hardly inspire confidence in a customer if the sales person has to keep referring to brochures all the time. Finally, it helps if you have good general knowledge. It keeps your intellect stimulated and alert, and gives you plenty of topics to engage your customers in when talking informally. It can also help to add a new perspective to problems and issues – a problem solved in a completely different industry might just be relevant in your own. Knowledge on its own will never close a deal – you need other sales skills as well – but if you cannot demonstrate that you understand not only what your product does but also what it can do for the customer, you will never develop the credibility and trust essential for closing a sale.

4. Contacts

This is a resource which it is impossible to over-value. The network of contacts that you develop and maintain during your career is a resource that will make the difference between average and outstanding success. Any customer you meet, any prospect you approach, any colleague you work with and any associates you team up with may be useful to you in the future. I'm not suggesting you 'collect' people solely for their value to you in business. I know a few sales people like that and they have no friends, just a long list of acquaintances, because they give the impression that they will exploit anyone if they think it will further their own ends.

What is important is that you keep tabs on who is moving where; that you maintain relationships with people you have worked with, even if it is on the most casual basis; and that your network of contacts is as wide as possible. Not because you will be constantly badgering any of them for business or a job, but because of the snippets of information, gossip even, that you can pick up. People like to know what is going on and a mutual exchange of information, even infrequently, is very welcome. People pop up in the most unlikely places and who knows if an old customer of yours might one day become the Managing Director of a new company – getting in to see him will be easier if you have dropped him a Christmas card every year or have given him a call every six months or so. This is not a cynical process. It must be genuine and sincere, but the very best sales people have an address book full of names, phone numbers and other contact information which is invaluable in helping them understand what is going on in their world.

External resources
External resources cover such a wide range of assets that it would be impossible to cover them all here. Nevertheless, a sales person will encounter and use the following widely, if not daily, throughout his career. Exploiting them to the full is essential to success:

1. Communications
Business communications include: telephones, mobile phones and text messaging, pagers, memos, voice mail, answering machines, video conferencing, messaging services, tape machines, letters, fax machines and e-mail. They are evolving and changing rapidly – faxes, for example, were only introduced a few years ago and already they are ubiquitous. Today there is no reason ever to be out of touch with your office and customers and, with new developments like e-mail and Internet access available directly from a mobile phone, the technology is making the ability to communicate and gather information ever easier.

Given the complexity of most of these devices, and the speed at which they develop, most people use only a fraction of the facilities available to them. Make sure you know how to use them to your advantage. Take time to store phone numbers in your mobile. Make sure you use a messaging service and alter your greeting every day so that, if you can't answer the phone immediately, the caller knows when you are likely to call back. **Always** return calls and never be tempted to use voice mail or answer phones as a call vetting tool. Make sure you turn mobiles off in meetings and restaurants – it is common courtesy and no-one likes the interruptions – and remember that anyone can be listening if you use a phone in public. Don't be tempted to use fancy ringing tones that play a tune – it might impress or amuse someone for about five minutes. You only have to travel on a train during the rush-hour to know how infuriating mobile phones can be – and most of the calls are completely trivial.

Make sure you turn mobiles off in meetings and restaurants.

Don't ignore the older forms of business communication. Letters are essential for prospecting and they can be a very personal way of establishing relationships with customers. The fax and e-mail are an acceptable alternative to letters in some cases and are excellent tools for keeping in touch or for confirming information quickly. Always confirm verbal arrangements, agreements and understandings in writing, whether by letter, fax or e-mail. Never be tempted to lapse into sloppy behaviour or informality. Spelling and grammar are just as important as in a letter. I've heard it said that, with e-mail, the message is more important than the medium and that spelling is unimportant. This is rubbish, especially with the spell checking and grammar tools available with modern applications. Humour can be acceptable, and no-one likes an overly formal or officious message, but remember that any letter, fax, e-mail, voice mail or memo can hang around to haunt you for a very long time. Never be tempted to voice anger or irritation in any written or recorded way. Remember that politeness is never out of place. Keep messages short and to the point – I have had people leave messages on my mobile that are so long the whole memory has been used up. And they still didn't finish their message! Don't waste your own or anyone else's time by using any method of communication incorrectly.

With e-mail, I know some people who hide behind the medium. They use the lack of personal contact to voice opinions or to give them an authority they would not have in a face to face, or even a telephone, conversation. Do not be tempted to hide in this way and if you can't say something to someone's face, don't say it at all. In many organisations people use e-mail instead of speech, even if the person they are contacting is just down the corridor. Selling is all about personal contact. Only use e-mail for gaining or disseminating information, or for confirming arrangements or agreements.

2. Information Technology

Information Technology is very closely associated with business communications, but includes additional facilities like computers, the Internet, extranets, intranets, computer applications and so on. The speed of change is again breathtaking and nearly everyone in business will have a PC on their desk and be expected to have at least a rudimentary understanding of word processing, spreadsheets, e-mail and databases. Being able to use the Internet is increasingly important, especially as e-business and e-commerce develop into stable platforms for business. Many companies are developing 'intranets' – internal company information services – and 'extranets' – information services limited to close partner and associate companies.

Again, sales people need to be able to use all of these facilities to their advantage and to keep up with developments. Many will be expected to produce their own letters and quotations, albeit with the support of company templates. In many companies additional applications like forecasting tools, customer tracking programmes (often called Customer Relationship Management or CRM) and the like will also be used. At their best, computer systems allow information to be typed in once and then disseminated and manipulated as required. At their worst they can be a very real barrier to business and it is as well to know that all systems, applications and the Internet will break down, often on a regular basis. Coping with these frustrations is essential and some sort of back up is no bad idea. For example, even though all my customer records are held electronically and a company wide planning system is in place, I still maintain a file of business cards and keep my old fashioned diary up to date. I know there is some duplication of effort, but it means I still have some control over what is going on when the computer fails.

The Internet is an essential source of information and it is amazing just what is available. The biggest problem is not in finding information, it is in coping with the quantity. There is so much information that it can be hard sifting through it to find exactly what you need, although there are an increasing number of applications and information services which will do the sifting for you, or automate the process.

Do not get sucked into believing that information technology is a real aid to productivity. Remember that we were promised the paperless office when the PC was launched? It hasn't arrived yet, and it probably never will. Shuffling bits of paper about and printing out documentation will be with us for the foreseeable future and it can be time-consuming. And so can the Internet. I've seen people become so engrossed in their 'research' that they forget the reason why they were looking for information in the first place. I've even heard people claim that playing Solitaire or Tetris on their PCs helps them to think better! Do not get dragged into this state of mind and remember that sales people can only sell something if they see a customer. Research is not selling, even if it is important.

3. Sales Aids
Sales aids cover such a wide range of tools and facilities that I am certain to miss a number out, but they include: overhead and slide projectors, sales presenters, white boards, flip charts, business cards, brochures, leaflets, technical documentation, demonstration systems, samples, reference visits, and so on. Anything the sales person can use to make the job of selling easier could be considered a sales aid, but a familiarity with those in the above list will be very useful to all. The main purpose of a sales aid is to help get a message across and to help underline quality and service. Being able to show or demonstrate what you are talking about is a very powerful means of communication and most of the above achieve this in one way or another.

If you do any sort of formal presentation, whether to customers or internally within your own company, the ability to use presentation equipment is essential. Whether you use overhead projectors with transparencies, slides and a 35mm projector or a PC connected to a projector, you must know how it all works. Make sure there are spare bulbs and that the screens are clean and not liable to fall over (I've seen it happen!). Have a contingency in mind if the technology fails (paper slides as a back up are a good idea). Keep a spare copy of your Microsoft Power Point™ slides on a disk if you use a PC. Make sure you practise your presentation in advance so that you are familiar with how it all works and, if several people are presenting, make sure slides and handovers are all prepared and practised before you give the presentation. Keep meeting rooms clean and tidy too – one sales person I used to work with polished the table and computer screens before important customer visits. I'm not suggesting you should go that far, but creating the right impression means attention to detail and ensuring everything works smoothly.

In some lines of business, a sales person will need to use a sales presenter or sample book to demonstrate key features of his product or service. These are valuable tools and being able to use them effectively will determine what sort of impression you make on the customer. That is not to say that you need to be overly slick or polished, but you do need to know where everything is, have it well organised and use a folder or binder that is easy to handle. I was in a shop recently watching a sales person flick through her presenter looking for technical information and prices for a specific product. She knew where everything was and got the infor-mation quickly, but there were many loose sheets and bits of paper in the presenter that fell on the floor and slipped out onto the counter. It didn't appear to upset the shop's propri-etor, but I couldn't help thinking about the problems the sales person would have in getting it all back into order again later on – that's if she managed to collect all the bits when she had finished! Sales presenters are peculiarly personal things and, even amongst sales people from the same company, there will be marked differences even when they are giving the same message. If you use a sales presenter or sample book make sure you are comfortable with it and rearrange things to provide meaning and support to your presentations, not someone else's.

White boards and flip charts are so ubiquitous that there is a tendency to forget their effectiveness in a wide variety of sales situations. In many cases, a white board gets used for an important meeting and someone scrawls on it – "Do not remove!" and it stays like that for months. Never leave information on white boards or flip charts – copy it down and then erase it. Conversely, in customer offices, check their white boards for important information – many managers forget they've written something down about strategy or structure – it becomes a bit like wallpaper – but it might be useful for you. White boards are very useful for capturing important details during brain-storming sessions or for sketch-ing out ideas which need to develop and grow as a discussion continues – the 'chalk and talk' approach. Flip charts can be used for major presentations, although writing everything out can be laborious and overheads slides or a Microsoft Power Point™ presentation are probably better for this. Flip charts come into their own, however, if you use them to capture ideas or points during a presentation. For example, you might start off the presentation asking each attendee what they hope to get out of the meeting and then recording it on the flip chart. At the end of the presentation you can go back and see if they got what they hoped for. Flip charts can also be useful for capturing objections or queries during the course of a presen-tation which you don't want to answer straight away, but which are too important to ignore. Both white boards and flip charts can be useful for helping to visualise a solution or simplify a complex idea – the 'picture paints a thousand words' approach.

Even simple business cards are valuable pieces of self promotion and should not be underestimated. They are also a handy record of the people you meet and can become a useful reference library of past customers and colleagues – don't throw them away. Brochures are very important too. They not only give an impression of the sort of company you work for, they also help to make the product or service you are offering more tangible for the customer. Never give out any form of documentation unless you know what it contains in detail – the customer will always ask questions. Never send out brochures or leave them for customers as a substitute for a face to face call. They are a useful aid in moving a sale forward, but they won't close a deal for you.

The same is true for demonstration systems, samples and reference visits. They won't close a deal on their own, but a good one will make success that much more certain. And I can guarantee they will lose you business if they are poor. Yet I have been with sales people who have dished out samples generously, impressing with their largess, but who never checked that the samples worked. And in one case they didn't. The sales person did not get the order. Everyone likes to get something for nothing, but not if it is shoddy, broken or past its sell-by-date. If you are using demonstration systems, make sure everything works and that there is some sort of contingency or fall back position if things go wrong (and they usually will if computers are involved!). If you are taking a prospect on a reference visit to an existing customer, take the time to brief the customer in detail on who is coming, what he hopes to see, what his agenda is, and so on. Work with him to ensure the visit is as trouble-free as possible for both parties. Never forget to thank the customer for his help afterwards and to keep him informed of the progress of the deal. Buy him lunch or some other token if the deal is closed.

4. Business Documentation

Again, I have listed a whole range of items here, all of which may seem somewhat mundane and matter of fact. And they are! But that doesn't make them any less important and you would be surprised at how many sales people use them poorly. They include: order pads, contracts, Terms and Conditions, customer records, account plans, diaries, day books, planners and reports, proposals and quotations, price books, references and testimonials.

You would have thought that order pads, contracts, terms and conditions, quotations, price lists and the like would all be second nature to every sales person. They should be, but they are not. There are some sales people who do not know their Terms and Conditions inside out and some who can't find their way around the price list. A facility with all of these items is a prerequisite for success. If you get to the stage where the customer is asking about contracts and conditions or is querying prices in detail, there is a very strong chance he is interested in buying. You will lose business if you fall down at this last hurdle. It is in your best interests to know everything there is to know about these items, and to keep on top of changes and amendments. For example, don't keep old price lists in your file. Throw them away and print out new ones, otherwise you stand the chance of giving the customer the wrong information. If the customer has to sign something, make sure you take a pen that works and you have plenty of copies of everything. A spare order pad may take up space in your bag, but how are you going to feel if the customer agrees to sign and you find you used your last order form up last week and have none left!

Quotations are legally binding, even if made verbally, and

they should never be given lightly. In many cases they have to be prepared in advance and they often take the form of a proposal. If you are involved in answering Tenders, then the proposal assumes an even greater importance because it is often the only chance you will have of addressing the prospect's requirements. It is also legally binding. Sales proposals are very important documents and in some organisations they employ dedicated Bid Managers to produce them. Nevertheless, a proposal is first and foremost a sales document and the sales person must be involved in every aspect of its production, even if he doesn't physically have to do all of the work. It must look and read well and it must deliver a coherent message that supports the whole sales campaign. It is true that the first thing the prospect will look at is the price, but he will also notice the quality of what he has been given and will ultimately judge your company on it.

5. Advertising and marketing

In many companies, advertising and marketing are the responsibility of specialist departments, although sales people are often involved in some of the activities. Advertising, direct mail and other marketing activities cover a wide range of enterprises, all designed to promote the company's products and services to the widest possible audience. In some cases, these will generate real leads to follow up, but in general, most advertising and marketing is designed to promote a general awareness of your company and its products. Whatever your company is doing, you should be aware of it and have the latest documentation and information to hand just in case a prospect sees something and asks you questions. Although the sales person himself does not have much input into these items himself, they can be very useful to him in the wider scheme of things.

Exhibitions, seminars, trade fairs, conferences and the like can also be a very effective way of promoting a company's products and services. Sales people are often employed directly in manning stands or providing support. Knowing what to do in such circumstances and how to use the various pieces of equipment is obviously important. But maintaining a professional approach at all times is also key. They can be very good ways of gaining up to date information about the competition and for keeping tabs on colleagues and associates who have moved to different companies. They can also be very useful for keeping abreast of market trends and emerging technologies. As a method of lead generation they can be useful too, but they can be very expensive and some companies only exhibit because a failure to do so would be even more costly in terms of the negative comments occasioned by their absence.

6. Sources of information

Information is the stock-in-trade of the sales person and comes from a multiplicity of sources – dealers, distributors, partners, colleagues and customers, libraries, trade press, newspapers, journals, reports, directories, telephone books, report and accounts and the Internet. As a resource, information of any kind is invaluable, helping with prospecting, market and business knowledge, the success of the competition and how your own company is perceived in the marketplace. I have already covered some of this elsewhere, but one tip that I have always found useful is to get hold of a customer's or prospective customer's Annual Report and Accounts. All public companies publish an annual report by law. Many publish them on the Internet or they are freely available from the marketing department or the Company Secretary. They are an invaluable source of information on the company's financial state and strategic focus, as well as who comprises the Board of Directors, other companies within the group, senior managers and so on. It helps if you have a rudimentary understanding of balance sheets because there is a wealth of information in the figures, but all of the supporting information is also extremely useful. For example, the Report and Accounts usually detail the company's Corporate Goals and Mission Statements, and it can be very effective to refer to these in a presentation, especially if you are trying to show how your products and services could support the prospect's strategic aims.

Resources – a personal perspective

One resource that I find invaluable is a daybook. I use a simple A4 hardback book to record everything that I do on a daily basis. Not in some overly fastidious way, but just to note down the actions taken at meetings, phone calls made and their results, contact information, notes from training courses and seminars, details of customer visits, sales meetings, and so on. This builds up into a very valuable document over time and, although I may transfer the information into other formats, the daybook still forms a very useful reference document. Before meetings I jot down whom I will be seeing and my main objectives for the meeting, and I do the same with phone calls. I also keep a running list of actions I need to complete and information I need to find out.

In the past, I used to write things down on scraps of paper or use a pad, but pages often went missing or (especially in my case) became so illegible that such records were useless over time. A daybook forces you to be neater and tidier, as well as forming a permanent record of what you have done on a daily basis. Many of these items will be tied in with the daily objectives noted in my diary as part of my personal planning process, but it also allows me to record anything ad hoc that occurs, as well as to draw up a list of actions for the next day.

Here is a sample page from my current daybook:

Tuesday 2nd May 2XXX

Actions:

1. Phone xyz company to chase information for proposal.
2. Send quote to abc company for new e-commerce products.
3. Book tickets for flight from Heathrow next Wednesday – arrange taxi too.
4. Phone John at consultants to check on his understanding of market status – meeting?
5. See Gill at energy company with invites for forthcoming seminar.
6. Cold call the next three companies on my prospect list.

1. John from consultants phoned with date for meeting – 10:30, 9th May at their offices in London. Mentioned abc co definitely favour us and have dropped evaluation of rival product. Still have to do demo though and send quote. He believes market sees us as a very strong contender, would like to arrange joint seminar for their customers – discuss further at meeting.

2. abc quote finished and e-mailed. Follow up next Tuesday.

3. Tickets booked – flight BA 1234, leave 07:30 arrive 08:35, flight BA 4321 return 18:30 arrive 19:35. Paid credit card. Tickets for collection at departure.

4. Discussed sales forecast with Sales Manager – new Q3 commission multiplier [an additional commission incentive in the third quarter of the financial year] available – try and pull abc deal into August if possible.

5. Discussion with Sales Director at xyz company. Their requirements seem to be changing all the time. New name to contact – John Smith 01234 567890. Phone him when he gets back from holiday on 5th to check requirements.

6.   Cold calls –
     1.   Not available – call back tomorrow.
     2.   Have rival product, not interested, but send relevant infor-
          mation (sent).
     3.   Meeting arranged for 20th June with Marketing Director,
          letter of confirmation sent along with invite to executive
          briefing in Birmingham on 15th.

Meeting

Gill Porter   energy company   02/05/XX
Shaun Sheppard

         Ask her about   1. Timescales.
                           2. Budget.
                           3. Decision making process.

Gill not the decision maker, but a key advisor. Gave me organisation
chart and recommended I see Gail Pinder, Purchasing Director and Peter
Smith, IT Manager. In her opinion, the FD would almost certainly get
involved too – check. Decision will be made by the end of July – need
solution in by September.

Budget has been allocated, although she wouldn't say how much.
Clearly evaluating our two main rivals as well as others. Noticed
proposal on her desk from that new company – suss them out on the Net
(done – very niche player, look under-capitalised, but products appear
very impressive – if they can deliver!).

Gill plays golf – provide invite to next corporate golf day.

In her opinion, they really need e-commerce functionality, especially
the ability to provide targeted e-mail campaigns to their existing
customer base, and to give them an opportunity to order over the web.
Links into their call centre would be an advantage too. Told her we can
do all of this and more – left brochure.

Left invites to seminar – she says she will come with Peter Smith,
but send him an invite anyway – done.

5

CLOSING

What is closing?

There is only one way to be successful as a sales person and that is to bring in the order – not once, but again and again and again. To achieve this, the professional needs to target business he can win and then be effective in closing it. To many, the ability to close a sale is considered a black art and there are plenty who see 'the close' as the most worrying aspect of their job. Over time this has given rise to a whole range of 'sure-fire' techniques for winning business and, at the last count, there were well over one hundred recognised ways of closing a sale. I don't know about you; trying to remember them all would be hard enough, but deciding which one to use in any given sales situation would be way beyond me! It seems that there is an over-emphasis on 'the close' as being the most important ability a sales person can master. All too often it is seen as some sort of trick to get the customer to place an order rather than a legitimate request for the business. In my experience top sales people very rarely have to resort to tricks or stratagems because, by the time they get to the point of asking for the order, the customer is already in a position to sign the contract.

Now, I'm not suggesting that 'closing' is a last resort used by poor sales people to make up for a poor sales process.

Closing is a reality and an essential skill. But, to see it as the only way to win business is to limit your chances of success. When I defined selling in chapter 1 of this book I said that selling is: *the process of establishing trust in your ability to recommend a solution to customers' needs or desires and helping them to invest in your recommendations.* If you establish yourself as being trustworthy, that you understand the customer's requirements thoroughly, that you can demonstrate how your solution will satisfy those requirements and how an investment in your proposals will be beneficial, asking for the order should be simple. If you get the whole process right, there will be much less need to trick, cajole, coerce or wrestle the customer into submission at the end.

Closing is the process of persuading a customer to make a commitment. Of getting him to say yes to your proposals rather than no. 'No' is something sales people hear an awful lot during their careers but, if the whole closing process is handled correctly, the chances of hearing 'no' will be reduced. The first thing to understand is that closing is **not** something that happens at the end of the sale – yes, you do have to ask for the order eventually – but it isn't a one-off activity that is confined to the last meeting in the sales process. In many senses closing *is* the sales process and, for me, it covers five key activities:

1.   When prospecting, look for opportunities that you can win. You must be very wary of anything where the decision-making process is vague or woolly, where the requirements do not fit your product or service mix, or where the competition have a much better chance than you. You will evaluate each opportunity very carefully and only 'close' on those which you have the best chance of winning.

2.   Once you have identified a good opportunity, any point in the sales process where you need the customer to do

something in your favour involves closing. From your initial telephone call you close the customer to get his commitment to a meeting. From that meeting you close him to gain commitment to a presentation. From the presentation you close him to accept a proposal. And so on until you close him to place an order.

3. Once you start to talk to customers, every word, action and deed is part of the closing process. You must be constantly aware of the customer's requirements and continually check and confirm you are providing him with all the information he requires to make a decision. You will also keep probing to make sure there are no hidden doubts or fears lurking in the background which could pop up at the last moment to scupper the deal. You will develop trust by completing every action you commit to. To put it crudely, you are 'softening the customer up' so that, when you do ask for the business, he cannot say ''I need some more time to think'' or ''I need to refer this to someone else''. You will already have given him the time, made sure he is the decision-maker and generally made him feel comfortable that your offering is what he needs.

4. You do need, formally, to ask for the order when you have confirmed that the customer is totally happy with your proposals and you have ensured that there is nothing else left unanswered or unresolved. If you don't round things up and ask for the order, or if you leave things dangling in the air, the customer has to decide what to do next for himself. Which is inevitably dangerous for you.

5. No matter how well you run the sales process, there will always be customers who need to to be reminded at the last moment that yours is the best offering and that they should place the business with you. Perhaps they doubt their own ability to make a decision. Perhaps they feel

the need for a little time to mull things over. Perhaps there really is a lingering doubt which needs to be cleared up. Whatever the reason, it is at this point that 'closing techniques' will be appropriate. I have detailed some of the most commonly used techniques below.

Closing techniques

Always use these with sensitivity. No two sales opportunities are the same and there can be no magic technique that will work in every sales situation. For example, if you are selling to a professional buyer, he will almost certainly have been on every training course going and will see any 'closing technique' coming a mile away. He is likely to get irritated very quickly if you try and pressurise him into making a decision. He may even take the view that you are too naive to deal with and cancel the meeting! Conversely, some customers are extremely vague and find it hard to make a decision of any kind. Closing them hard so that they feel pressured into making a decision can sometimes be a blessing in disguise. Otherwise they keep running around in circles and never quite face up to moving things forward.

1. **The trial close.**   This technique can be useful for helping to unearth hidden doubts or problems, or for helping to understand the decision-making process.

Sales person: ''You say you will need a bespoke widget –
                   if I demonstrate that we can provide a
                   bespoke widget to your satisfaction, will you
                   place an order with us?

Customer: ''Well, it would help, but our financial control-
                   ler might need to check your leasing rates and I
                   would certainly want to talk to another cus-
                   tomer of yours with a similar application.''

2. **The direct close.** This isn't really a technique, just a direct request for the order. Many sales people are afraid to come out and ask for the business, but it is their right. After all, they have spent time and effort on the customer and have a right to know where they stand. If the answer is 'yes' make sure you can advise the customer on how to proceed. Ideally have your order pad to hand or a contract ready for signing. If the answer is 'no', you have the right to ask why. It may just be a misunderstanding, or some hidden doubt rising to the surface. In which case address it and then close again.

Sales person: "I believe that covers all of your outstanding queries. Are you happy to proceed now? All I need is an order number from you and I can prepare the paperwork."

Customer: "Fine! You mentioned before you would need an order number, so I got purchasing to issue one in advance. Do I have to sign something as well?"

OR

Customer: "I'm not so sure. I need a bit of time to think about it."

Sales person: "I'm sorry to hear that. You agreed we had answered all of your queries. Is there something which is still unclear?"

Customer: "I guess I'm still a bit uncertain about your leasing terms."

Sales person: "I'd be pleased to run through them again. If I can clear things up to your satisfaction, would you then be happy to go ahead?"

Customer: "Fine! Just remind me why it has to be a five year lease, not three."

3. **The alternative close.** If the customer appears to like what he has seen, but seems to be unable to make up his mind and needs a bit of a nudge, offer him some simple alternatives to consider. By giving the customer a choice, his agreement to one of them implies that he has agreed to buy the product itself. It takes any pressure out of the process and makes the purchasing decision easier.

Sales person:	"I think that covers everything. Do you want to rent the solution or will you buy it outright?"
Customer:	"Our capital budget is depleted, we'll take the rental option."

OR

Sales person:	"I think that covers everything. Credit card or cash?"
Customer:	"I really like what you said, but I'm not sure . . ."
Sales person:	"I understand; it is a big commitment. Did I tell you we do it in two colours, blue or red. Which would you prefer?"
Customer:	"Oh, a blue one please."

4. **The assumptive close.** This technique attempts to get around the need for a customer to make a decision by assuming he has already done so. The sales person takes control of the situation and takes the pressure off the customer, which can be very useful in situations where the customer obviously likes what he has heard but finds it hard to make a decision.

Sales person:	"I believe that covers everything, when would you like delivery?"

OR

Sales person: "From what you have said, this investment fund really does seem to be right for you. Complete this banker's order and I'll set things up immediately."

5. **The recommendation close.** In some circumstances your ability to establish trust and build a strong relationship with the customer will see you acting as much as an advisor as a sales person. In such circumstances, the customer will expect you to recommend a way forward. Clearly you can only arrive at such a situation by displaying a high degree of integrity, but the ability to tell the customer what to do is something the very best professionals achieve on a significant number of occasions.

Customer: "That all seems pretty clear, but I'd like to know which one you believe is right for us."

Sales person: "Well, in my opinion, the straight repayment approach is more suited to your current circumstances."

Customer: "Fine! That's what we'll do then. Can we complete the paperwork now?"

6. **The 'desperation' close.** Sometimes customers will be determined not to make immediate decisions. They agree that they like what they have heard or seen and confirm that they are definitely going to purchase something. It may well be your product, but they just want to go home and mull things over for a while. All sales people know that it is much better to close a deal immediately rather than let the customer off the hook – they rarely come back – so the 'desperation' close might be worth trying, especially if you know there is a little more room for negotiation anyway.

Sales person:	"I think we are agreed this car fits your specification and your budget. Can we proceed with the paperwork?"
Customer:	"You're right, the car really fits the bill, but, as I said earlier, I don't want to make a decision now. I'd like to think it over for a day or two."
Sales person:	"I quite understand, but as you've made the effort to come to the showroom today and have invested quite a lot of time in looking at the options, is there anything else I could do to help you make a decision now?"
Customer:	"Well, an extra 10% discount would go a long way to helping me make up my mind."
Sales person:	"That's a bit of a tall order! I'll have to check with head office first. I'm happy to do that, but assuming they give the go ahead, will you place the order now? The first thing they will ask me is whether this is serious."
Customer:	"If you can stretch to the extra 10%, I'll be happy to sign up now."

7. **The lost sale or last chance close.**   In some situations the prospect will always say no. It may seem to you that there is no particular reason for this – you've answered all of the queries and your solution looks as if it would suit him – but he is adamant that he is not going to order from you. In reality you have lost the business, so you have really got nothing to lose. In the vast majority of cases, this approach will still draw a blank, but, occasionally, it might just persuade a customer to reopen discussions.

| Sales person: | "Well, I'm sorry we couldn't do business together. We've both spent a lot of time on this. Tell me, was there anything I could have done differently to have persuaded you to say 'yes'?" |

More about closing

All of the above techniques work and thousands of sales people use them as a matter of course to close business every day. They work because they are common sense. They are not tricks or magic charms, but ways of helping the customer to make a decision. With over one hundred such techniques to choose from I have only included the ones that I know work, either from observation or experience. That is not to say that the others don't work, or that you haven't got half a dozen other closing techniques up your sleeve which work well for you. However, there is much, much more to closing than these techniques. I have already outlined my belief that closing is a continuous process that starts well before you meet the customer and that you make the chances of success that much easier if you manage the whole sales process professionally. But there is even more to it than that. Closing is all about making the prospect say 'yes' to your proposals and, in a pressurised sales environment, you rarely have the luxury of time to consider your options. You often have to think on your feet rather than 'scientifically' choosing or planning how to proceed. With this in mind, here are some additional tips to help you close more successfully:

1. If a customer has an urgent requirement and you can demonstrate that your offering will satisfy this need conclusively, you won't need to worry about 'closing' to get the order. The sale will almost close itself if you remain sensitive to his needs. But be aware that you can snatch defeat from the jaws of victory in such circumstances, so don't oversell, become arrogant or push too hard when he is ready to buy. A failure to recognise buying signs costs sales people vast amounts of business, yet a degree of sensitivity and a recognition that each sales situation is unique is sometimes all that is required to be successful. Following some rigid 'closing plan' is not always appropriate.

2.   If tenders or formal purchasing procedures are involved, customers may award you the business without the need to close. They haven't spent their time telling you the problem they need resolving, and then listening to you trying to convince them that your product or service fits the bill, just for the fun of it. They need to resolve the problem and will buy something from someone. If you have established your credentials and made it onto the short-list, then you are obviously being seriously considered for the business. In some cases, the decision-making criteria will be published and each bidder will be scored against it. The supplier with the best score wins. There will probably be little need to close, but negotiations will be intense and things may break down. If you were second, don't assume all is lost until the contract has been signed.

3.   Your pressures are not the customer's pressures. No matter what demands you are under or time scales you are working to, these must not be transmitted to the customer. Desperation or stress will cause you to act irrationally or ignore the customer's requirements in favour of your own. This is guaranteed to lose you business because the customer will feel that his concerns are not being taken seriously and he will resent the additional pressures you put him under.

4.   When the solution to a customer's requirement is available from a number of suppliers, all offering virtually the same thing at similar prices, ask the customer how he will make the decision. Service, delivery, billing, the on-going relationship may all come into it. If the price and specifications are similar, help the buyer to make a decision by concentrating on other aspects where you can really claim an advantage.

5.   In order to get a commitment, the sales person must make it easy for the prospect to say yes. And if the

prospect does say no, the sales person must be able to come back and rephrase his request in such a way that a yes is more likely. Giving up just because the prospect doesn't say yes at once will lose you valuable business. Perseverance is the key to success. Until the order is awarded to someone else, you always have a chance to secure the business for yourself. Perceived wisdom has it that a sales person will hear 'no' at least five times on average in a sales campaign before getting a 'yes'.

6. In some cases it becomes apparent that, despite your best efforts, customers are clearly wasting your time. Whether there really is business there or not, walk away. Don't be tempted to be aggressive or unpleasant, even if they have really led you up the garden path, but do make it clear (politely!) that you value your time and will not be spending any more of it on them. Such circumstances are rare, but they do occur and the opportunity to walk out on a prospect for legitimate reasons can be very good for your self-confidence and self-esteem.

7. Never forget the power of silence. Once you have asked for the business do not be tempted to carry on speaking. In asking for the business you are asking a question. Do not say anything else until the customer has answered. This may seem difficult and a few seconds silence can seem like an eternity, but it puts the buyer on the spot and forces him to make his mind up. If you interrupt, it lets him off the hook. Don't forget, however, that many customers have been trained in techniques like this. Try it on a professional buyer and you might sit there for an hour waiting for one of you to crack!

8. It is also worth noting that many customers are increasingly sophisticated, so don't be surprised to find them

using closing techniques on you: "If you can give me a 50% discount on your prices, then I'll definitely buy!" Make sure you know how to handle such a situation should it arise.

9. The Elevator Pitch. This is a sales technique much practised in America. It may seem a bit of a cliché, but it is in fact a very useful discipline, helping you refine your approach and isolate the key messages that will be relevant to your prospect. Imagine that you are in a lift on your way to a major presentation with a key customer. The lift stops at the second floor and the customer's chief executive gets in. You have the time between him getting in and you getting out for your meeting to give him a quick presentation, résumé or pitch (call it what you will) on what you can do for his company. This may seem contrived, but unless you have a clear and succinct idea of the messages you want to deliver to your customer – the reasons why they should buy from you – you may not be effective in getting your ideas across. Visualising such a discussion in the 60 seconds you might have with a CEO in a lift might just help.

10. The 'gin and tonic' technique. Again, this might seem a bit of a sales cliché, but it is still a useful way of securing additional business. It takes its name from the fact that most people will buy some tonic water when they buy a bottle of gin. With a little imagination, the technique can be applied in a variety of situations to encourage customers to add to their order, for example: selling insurance or extended warranties to someone who has just bought a car; selling a printer or scanner to someone who has just purchased a PC; or selling training to someone who has just purchased a new software solution. When you think about it, the technique could be applied anywhere and can be used as an extra negotiating point or lever for closing an order.

What to do with objections and queries

Objections are an inherent part of the sales process. No sale will take place without a customer querying some of your claims or objecting to some of your proposals. Whether it is over price, fear of making a decision, a need for reassurance or suspicion, a customer will need to be satisfied that all of his objections are answered satisfactorily before he will commit to an order. Objections are proof that your customer is alive and well and listening to what you are saying. They are feedback on your handling of the sales process and should be welcomed. They give you an indication of where you have failed to probe deeply enough or where you have rushed through things with insufficient explanation. If the customer doesn't object, it doesn't mean that he has no objections, but getting them out into the open will be a problem. By voicing his concerns, the customer makes it easier for you to see where you need to spend more time and effort.

There is a lot you can do to prevent objections in the first place, although you will never stop them altogether. You can also deliberately provoke them so that you get them out in the open early. All of this takes planning. From past experience you will know what aspects of your offering usually cause concerns to your customers and you will have already developed effective ways of dealing with them. You can also make a shrewd guess that things like pricing, delivery, terms and conditions and proof of your claims will also need addressing at some stage, so make sure you are well prepared to deal with them should they arise. You must be able to justify your claims and proposals in detail and have evidence to back them up if necessary.

Objections need to be handled with sensitivity and tact. The last thing you need is an argument. Make sure you are relaxed and acknowledge that the customer has every right to question and query what you say. After all, a successful sale is based on trust and what better way to foster it than through the mutual exchange of views. It doesn't mean you have to accept what he says, but you must acknowledge his right to say it and demonstrate your complete understanding. If you are unclear what is wrong or why the customer is unhappy, spend whatever time is necessary in finding out. Don't make it an issue, but make sure you get it all out in the open before you attempt to address it. And once you have addressed it, make sure the customer is happy with your response and that the issue is put to bed. You do not want the same objection to rise up again further down the line.

Handling objections is all about listening. As the old saying says, "Lend half an ear to a question and you'll only give half an answer", and that is no good to anyone. If you do not understand what the objection is about and why the customer is objecting, you will not be able to address it in a way that will neutralise it. The objection will sit there unresolved and will become a bone of contention. It will affect the rest of the sales process – usually to your detriment.

Negotiation

As sure as eggs is eggs, there will be some haggling between you and the customer before the deal is actually closed. Professional buyers will not be satisfied until the pips squeak (or you make them feel they have bled you dry) and even your average customer will 'want a deal'. Customers feel better about making a purchase if they believe that they got a better deal out of you than anyone else. Today, so many sales people offer discounts and deals in the hope of making a sale that customers now never accept any price at face value. They expect there to be some room for negotiation.

The nature and type of negotiation will depend very much on the type of business you are trying to close. If you sell goods to a wholesaler, he will only be interested in how cheaply he can buy. Delivery and quantity might come into it, but his main concern will be to keep his margins as high as possible and that means buying from you as cheaply as possible. As a supplier to the wholesale trade, you will know what the customer expects and will price your goods accordingly. You would give greater discounts for larger quantities or regular deliveries, but would have clearly defined parameters to work within. If you are selling a complex IT solution to a large corporate company, where you would be seeking to develop the relationship over the long term, price will be only one of the items for negotiation. Service level agreements, maintenance, delivery, support, special billing or leasing agreements, bespoke contract terms – the list can be endless – are all subject to negotiation and very little is fixed. You might even need to involve a special team of people to help draw up the negotiated agreement!

However, whether you are selling simple products or immensely complex solutions, negotiating is always the same – the customer needs to buy something but wants a deal (or something for nothing if he can) and the sales person wants to close the sale, but doesn't want to 'give the shop away' in the process. As a Managing Director once pointed out to me when he rejected my request for extra discount to help close a deal, "Shaun, anyone can 'sell' anything to anyone if they give it away!" If you set a precedent by selling too cheaply, you will never be able to improve your margins in the future. As so much of selling is based on repeat business and long term relationships, this is the worst practice possible and should be avoided at all costs.

For me, there are five basic principles in negotiating:

1. Concentrate on the value of the overall solution to the customer, rather than the cost of the individual products or services of which it is comprised. If the customer values what you are selling, he will be prepared to pay for it.

2. Always look for the win:win scenario (a cliché I know, but it really is the most satisfactory way to negotiate) – a situation where both sides give a bit, but gain a lot.

3. Trade extras and add-ons instead of concentrating solely on price. Never give anything away needlessly. Make sure the customer understands the value of any such item before agreeing to trade it, or give it away. If an item is perceived as having little or no value to the customer, it has no negotiating value either.

4. Set your ultimate fall back position and stick to it regardless. Walk away if necessary. Getting up and walking away does not mean you cannot go back later on and it demonstrates to the customer how far you can and cannot go.

5. Never reveal desperation. If you appear too keen to complete a deal and the customer senses you would discount very heavily in order to close it, he will make you do just that. Never give in too easily, even if both sides know it is a bit of a game. Even in the most settled of business relationships, negotiation is a professional procedure and should never be taken lightly.

In many situations today customers are well aware that, in order for a sales person to do business and for his company to provide the level of support the customer requires, his company must make a profit. They don't want him profiteering, but they accept the principle that a profit must be made. With this in mind, negotiating in certain circumstances has started to take on a different flavour than in the past, although the various elements included below will still need to be negotiated very hard:

1. Open book accounting – where the company providing the solution will reveal on request exactly what their costs are in providing a solution and what level of profit they are making.

2.   Cost plus pricing – often closely associated with 1 above, where the company providing the solution agrees to charge only the cost of the solution plus a fixed profit margin to the customer.

3.   Shared risk/reward partnerships – often considered in new areas where the risks associated with a particular project are high, but where the rewards are high too. Both the customer and the supplier agree to share the positive and/or negative aspects of the project. For example, it might cost a supplier £100,000 to develop a solution for a particular customer, but, with that solution in place, the customer expects to generate some £500,000 of profit. The two companies agree that the supplier will not charge the full cost of the solution to the customer (say 30%), so as not to overburden them at the early and delicate stages of the project, in return for a percentage of the profits later on (say 20%).

Such arrangements have been developed to help foster healthy working partnerships where any worry about excess profits is removed from the equation so that both parties can concentrate on getting on with the business. Partnerships are often seen as extremely valuable in today's fast moving and ever changing marketplace and the ability to negotiate such agreements can be a very useful closing tool.

Unique Selling Points

All sales people are taught early on in their careers to capitalise on their Unique Selling Points (their USPs), i.e. the features, benefits, skills or services which their offering or company can claim to provide and which are unique to them. These USPs can help to swing a sale, or a negotiation, in your favour if the prospect sees them as being particularly beneficial and recognises that they are unavailable elsewhere. The sales person is therefore taught to present these USPs as a key differentiator in the sales campaign and to try and get the decision made on them rather than on more mundane issues.

This is a valid and powerful sales approach, but remember that USPs are only of any value if:

- They truly are unique.
- You can substantiate them.
- The customer really does perceive them as beneficial to him.

It is no good claiming your widget is unique because it is twice as fast as the opposition's when it isn't. The customer will expect proof before he buys and will kick you out if you are unable to substantiate your claims. He will also be unimpressed if, say, speed is less important to him than reliability.

The most successful sales people use USPs to their advantage in all sales and negotiating situations. They develop a list of key attributes which make their offering stand out from the crowd, even if their product is mundane or ordinary. For example, they might be selling photocopiers and theirs is little different from anyone else's, except for the fact that their maintenance contract will allow them to wheel in a replacement machine if the original breaks down and cannot be fixed within an hour. If no-one else offers such a service, the skilled sales person will introduce this as a key differentiator. While all the other suppliers will try and convince the customer that their machine has the cheapest cost per page, the greatest reliability, the least cost of ownership, 'our' sales person will cover all of these items to the customer's satisfaction, but he will major on the fact that the customer should never have more than 60 minutes down time, no matter what problems arise. In many cases, especially when comparing a number of products of similar price and specification, a customer can have real trouble making a decision – nearly all of the products on offer can do the job, so how does he choose? That unique selling point might just do the job for you.

One other point worth remembering is that your greatest and most powerful USP is **you**. I have already mentioned that people buy from people and this is an area where you, personally, can have the greatest impact on the sales process. You might be selling a very similar product to a number of other suppliers, but, if your customers see you as the key differentiator, then you will sell more than the opposition. Good service, being fun to work with, breadth of knowledge, empathy, 'going that extra mile', trust and integrity – anything which can make you stand out from the pack and make you seem a better person to do business with will help you win more business than anyone else.

6

PEOPLE

Why do people buy?

People buy things for two reasons – they either have a need for something or they desire something. Needs fall into a wide range of categories: you need to eat so you must buy food; if the washing machine wears out you need to get another one; if your competitor buys a computer system that improves his perform-ance, you need not only to keep up but also to try and go (at least) one better. If people need something, unless that need is urgent or desperate (and often even then), they will have a tendency to take some time over the decision. They will research the best price, compare specifications and performance and generally look for a good deal. They have to purchase something so they might as well get the most that they can for the money.

Desires, on the other hand, are more about gratification and aspirations than simple need. You might need a new car, but desire a Ferrari. A Ford will do the job just as well, but the Ferrari has the aspirational quality that places it way above the mundane. The fact that you might never be able to afford one is just part of the mystique. If people desire something, they are much less likely to query the price or to haggle. The decision becomes much more emotional. They frequently buy on impulse and the sales person's job is less about selling and much more about helping them to buy.

Emotional appeal

You may feel that this is 'intellectualising the bloomin' obvious'; that it is all just common sense. And it is! But that doesn't mean that all sales people understand it, or use it to help them sell more effectively. People like to buy, but they don't really like to be 'sold' to. Think how you react to the flash 'wham-bam' sales pitch, the pushy shop assistant or the overly smooth patter of a financial adviser. Is it any wonder that many people are intrinsically cynical about estate agents and car salesmen? We have all been let down or disappointed by sales people who promised a lot but delivered little. And this is often because they have not spent some time trying to understand what it is we need or want. They have just launched into their spiel or tried to push us in the direction of the item that generates the most commission without finding out our real requirements.

Most people want to be treated with courtesy and respect: to be helped to buy. This means being given informed advice on the options open to them, based upon a thorough understanding of what it is they want. Understanding and empathy are involved, but perhaps even more importantly, there needs to be enthusiasm too. As you get to understand what it is the customer really wants, you can start to align your offering with their needs while also stimulating their desire. The very best sales people exhibit so much enthusiasm for their products or services that the customer's need can be transformed into a desire, even for things that seem mundane or ordinary.

Obviously, if you are selling, say, bricks to builders' merchants, their overwhelming concern will be price. They need bricks, but they will only buy them if the price is right. They have to protect their profit margins and they know what price they can sell the bricks on at in the open market. Stimulating a desire for bricks in such a situation is difficult (to say the least!). However, while there will be a stiff negotiation on price, the sales person can still use enthusiasm to his advantage. The bricks are a commodity, but the deal he can do for the builder's merchant will be special. Price, quantity, delivery times, call off capability, special offers, promotional items, joint advertising and marketing – the list is almost endless – can all be combined to produce an exciting offer which the sales person can encourage the builder's merchant to get enthusiastic about.

People like to feel that they have been treated specially, that they have been able to get something no-one else has received – a better price, the latest release, a one-off deal. They are also concerned if they feel that they might miss out on something – limited special offers or the chance to influence product development, for example. Your customers and prospects are human and will exhibit the same emotions as anyone else – fear of missing out, greed, pride, excitement – and all of these can be used to your advantage in the sales process. I am not suggesting that you manipulate your customers in a cynical way, far from it, but recognise that buying something is often an emotional decision, and use it to your benefit.

Buying – a personal perspective
This happened to me very recently. I needed a new car; something that would do long distances in comfort and could accommodate the family while still cutting a bit of a dash. I looked at BMW, Lexus, Mercedes and the like. I realised I couldn't afford a new one, but I felt I could get a very good deal on a late model, low mileage car. Unfortunately, despite the fact that the market is awash with cars, most sales people were determined to either treat me with disdain because I wouldn't buy a new car, or try and profiteer at my expense. I knew I would have to buy the car on finance, but I didn't want the salesman making a massive profit on the sticker price as well as making an even bigger profit out of the finance deal. Nearly every salesman I talked to started out asking me how much I had to spend a month. When I told them I wanted a

deal on the sticker price before I told them what my monthly budget was, they got defensive or lost interest. Not one of them asked me why I wanted their type of car or took an interest in my aspirations about owning a luxury vehicle. They thought they already knew and were only interested in what was in it for them.

Getting quite cynical about things, I approached a Jaguar dealer feeling rather irritable. The salesman let me wander about for a few minutes to get a view of his stock, rather than pouncing on me immediately (or ignoring me altogether as had happened at some dealers), and then he came to see me. I quickly told him my basic requirements, that I wanted a deal and that I was pretty disillusioned with car salesmen. He laughed, not at all put out. "But do you want a Jaguar?" he asked. "If you do, I can sell you one – and I can do you a deal – but I'd be happier knowing it is really what you want before we start talking about money". This was the first time I had been asked whether the make of car was important to me. Once we began talking I realised that I hadn't really decided, so long as it fitted my parameters, but the salesman was so enthusiastic about the quality and heritage of his cars that I couldn't help but become interested. He obviously noticed this, but didn't push the point. Instead he took me to a computer and proceeded to bring up his stock lists, including the cost prices. This was a bit of a revelation given how much higher the sticker prices were, but he said, "As you can see, Mr. Sheppard, there is some margin for negotiation here. I obviously have to make a profit and cover the costs of the guarantees and servicing we have already done on the cars, but I think you can afford something a bit better than you realise".

This was a very shrewd move on his part and the 'open-book' approach went a long way towards dispelling the latent cynicism I was feeling. Nevertheless, it wasn't quite out of my system and I made some comment about the swingeing interest rates he would charge me for finance. Quickly calling up another system, he asked me a few direct questions about what I was willing to pay for a car, as well as what interest rates I thought might be reasonable and then produced a detailed analysis of what my money might be able to buy me. "Given that information and the fact that I will only charge you cost plus a margin, rather than the sticker price, you can afford any one of these cars here" and he showed me several vehicles with sticker prices considerably in excess of my original budget. I tried not to show my surprise but these cars were virtually new and highly specified – very desirable in fact. Needless to say, a test drive confirmed exactly what the salesman had said in terms of comfort and performance, but I was already sold on the idea that I could afford a much better car than I thought I could. I bought one.

The salesman not only managed my initial antagonism, he used it to his advantage by cutting out any preamble or subterfuge and going straight to the heart of what I initially wanted – a deal. His facility with his support systems and his patient questioning and understanding of exactly what I wanted created a feeling of trust and his enthusiasm for the marque helped to underline what a good decision I would be making if I bought a Jaguar. However, although he knew I wanted a deal and was prepared to negotiate, he judged very shrewdly what it was I really wanted – the best car I could get rather than the very best deal. I ended up buying a car at the very top of my budget rather than well within it, and I was delighted. It was a good deal for both of us and, although I'm sure (with the benefit of hindsight!) there was more he was prepared to give away if I had haggled further, he made a profit and helped to keep stock moving in a sluggish market and I got something better than expected. A true win:win situation.

Three types of buyer
There are three categories of buyer who you are likely to meet in most sales situations. Each has different requirements and

buying criteria, but they may all have a bearing on the success or failure of your sales campaign:

1. **Decision Makers.** As the name implies, these are the people who will say yes or no to you. They have the authority to make a decision without recourse to anyone else and they will be held accountable to their organisation for their decisions. The decision maker may well be the person who owns the budget that this purchase will be funded from, but he may not. Decision makers will need to be convinced of the benefits of your offering to them and their organisation or department. They will analyse your proposals and compare them with their own requirements and views, as well as those of the users and advisors who may report to them or who may be affected by the purchase. Typically, decision makers are interested in productivity, bottom line performance and long term benefits – the bigger picture. They will place some emphasis on business partnerships and will be looking for a good match between your company and theirs, in addition to the specifics of your solution. From a financial view point they will be interested in the return on investment as much as the cost.

2. **Advisors.** Others who have an interest in or may be affected by the purchase may become involved in the decision-making process. Although they may be asked to make a recommendation they will not make the final decision; yet they may have a very strong influence on the outcome. Advisors will be interested in the specifics of the solution you are offering, particularly its functionality and capability, as well as its price and the total cost to their organisation. They will be analytical by nature and will need to see demonstrations and presentations. Typically, these are the people who will prepare tenders and specifications, evaluate proposals and eliminate the also-rans. They will almost certainly be tasked with negotiating with short-listed suppliers, not just on price,

but on delivery, maintenance, support, lead-times, and so on. Advisors will need to see that your product or service fits the parameters that they have been given. They will tend to work within certain set boundaries, rather than seeing the bigger picture, although it is possible to sell to their personal aspirations in some cases, especially if they are ambitious.

3. **Users.**   Anyone who will implement and use your solution, either on a daily or an ad hoc basis, could be classed as a user. Some of them may be involved in the evaluation process and may well comment on things like ease of use and relevance to their job, but they will typically be more interested in the impact on themselves than on the wider company. They will need to see that your solution helps them do their job better and makes things easier for them. On the whole, they will not be interested in price or detailed analysis, but they are likely to need hands-on demonstrations and reassurance about backup and support.

Managing politics and power
Whether we like it or not, politics are a reality in just about every organisation, and the larger the organisation, the more complex and involved the politics. The political structure of an organisation is much more informal than the established organisational structure, but it is at least as powerful. It may not be recognised in any overt way, but its influence can be considerable. For a sales person, recognising that politics play a part in some sales situations – especially the larger and more complex ones – can be a valuable insight, and the difference between success and failure. It doesn't mean that you have to get involved, and it is almost certainly better that you don't in an active sense, but recognising what is going on and noting who holds the real power in the organisation will help to ensure that you spend your time and effort on the most influential individuals.

Politics is all about power and influence and is a natural development in any human endeavour. People are ambitious and will seek to rise to positions of authority if they can. Politics are involved at a number of levels – the desire to be promoted, competition between individuals or departments, the fight for funding, the battle for resources – and it can help or hinder a sales campaign depending on how well you read the signals. The key to success is observing who has authority and who has influence. Those who have authority make decisions and place orders. Those who have influence affect what decisions are made and which orders are placed and with whom. A classic example would be the Managing Director's secretary. In the scheme of things she has little or no authority at all within the organisation, but her influence can be substantial because she has the MD's ear. He will often rely on her to organise his diary and to vet the people he sees. He may even seek out her opinion on certain things. Some secretaries hold more real power than senior managers and their patronage can be very valuable. Another potentially powerful person might be an external consultant. Again, he has no real authority within the organisation, but because he has been employed for his expertise and because the company is paying him (no doubt handsomely) for his services, his opinion will hold a lot of weight.

Discovering who has power and influence is a matter of understanding your accounts thoroughly, getting to know as many people as possible and observing who is well regarded and who isn't. This can only be achieved on an informal basis – direct questioning about who holds the real power in a company will never be answered satisfactorily. Look out for those people who always seem to be involved in major projects or decisions, whose names seem to crop up a lot in discussions or to whom others seem to defer. Management may delegate responsibility to certain junior but key individuals who have greater influence than their position might suggest. And there may be some 'rogue' individuals who appear to work against the tide at times, but who always seem to get what they want – for example, funding to take on a new member of staff when there is a general head-count freeze.

In selling to these influential people, the key is to demonstrate what your offering can do for them as much as for their organisation. That is not say that they are uninterested in what your offering can do for their company – far from it, because their long term career and aspirations depend on the company being successful. But, if they can be the ones to recommend the best solution, or drive through a decision against the odds that turns out to be the right one, their political capital and influence will increase. Promotion, influence, power and career development are just as important as profitability, productivity, competitive edge and innovation when selling in an overtly political environment. However, never make the mistake of openly selling to the political side of the business. It is too ill-defined and changes too easily. Those involved will never admit its existence either. Sell to the business drivers first and foremost. But when you do identify people of influence who are involved in the sales process, it may be possible to emphasise the more intangible benefits they might personally gain from recommending your solution. Be sensitive when doing so and do not allow yourself to become an active player (or a pawn) in some political power struggle.

An 'inside track' – a personal perspective
Obviously, selling to the decision maker is the most direct route to closing a sale and in many cases you will be able to do just that. However, in larger and more complex deals, you will find yourself dealing with a wide range of users and advisors and having them on your side is vital to success. I remember quite vividly a deal we were trying to close with a

major utility company. We had installed a small trial computer system which had performed faultlessly and all of the financial analysis for the purchase of the main system had been based on our costings. The Board signed off the business case and asked several companies to bid for the full-blown installation. We felt we were well placed, but continued to canvass the decision-makers, advisors and users to make sure we had covered all of their concerns. We put in a very keen price because the deal was potentially worth millions and we really wanted to win it after all the hard work and effort we had put in. We lost; even after we had flown the decision makers to our manufacturing plant in Scotland for a VIP visit and had involved our CEO to underwrite certain guarantees.

The reason we lost was simple. One of the technical advisors on the project had worked for a rival supplier for many years before joining the utility company. He maintained strong links with his past employer and fed them competitive data about all the other bidders. The decision makers relied on him heavily during the evaluation process. It was inevitable that his old company would win given such an inside track. I would never have known this information if it were not for another supplier. For the first and only time in a competitive situation I was phoned up by a rival salesman. His company had lost out too and he was pretty angry about it, having found out the information concerning the technical advisor by a back-door route. He felt both our companies had been 'stitched-up' and had just been used as a stick to beat the winning supplier with in order to get a better price. He was right, but there was nothing we could do about it. The order was placed and we had no proof. I doubt we could ever have got this information during the normal sales process, particularly as the advisor was acting in a highly questionable way, but it is a good, if extreme, example of just how powerful an inside track can be.

Teamwork

Your customers and prospects are not the only people you will have to work with, manage and, at times sell to, in your career. Colleagues, partners, associates, management, people from other areas of your company, suppliers – the list is endless – will all have a bearing on how successful you can be. The same principles of professionalism that you use with your customers apply no matter whom you are dealing with in business. If your colleagues and partners do not trust or respect you, their co-operation will be hard to sustain.

Most sales people are self-sufficient and tend to pride themselves on their ability to 'do it all'. Unfortunately, the days of an individual sales person being able to manage all aspects of a sale are rapidly disappearing in many industries. Too often, the one who tries to 'do it all' will only do some of it well and, given the competition, there is an increasing need to do everything well. A sales person's primary role is to sell and he can only do this when he is seeing customers. Sorting out delivery issues, administration, technical support, customer service etc. may all have a bearing on how well he can do his job, but, in many cases, he will be unable to do all of it properly and sell as well. This means delegation. The sales person will certainly want to be kept informed of what is going on and he will want to make sure that everything is done, not only to the exacting standards he expects, but also to the customer's satisfaction. But, by letting people who are more skilled at these specific tasks undertake them, he gives himself more time to get on with what he is really paid to do – sell.

Taking responsibility for a team of people, or delegating tasks which you have previously been responsible for, can seem daunting. Sales people rarely have line management responsibility for staff and resources are often scarce, even in the most successful of companies. Ensuring that the right people work on your opportunities – people who believe in the same principles of customer service that you do and who complement your own abilities – is a matter of professionalism, sales ability and communication. In fact, the same mix of skills and abilities you would use with your customers and prospects. You will have to sell your opportunities to these people so that they share your enthusiasm and belief in the value of the business they are working on. They must want to work with you and enjoy it because your sales colleagues will be continually vying for their services.

Every company will be different in this respect and the range of tasks a sales person will be expected to undertake will vary enormously. If you are in a position to delegate certain things, or can work with a team of people to a common end – an order! – the following principles apply:

1. Be professional at all times.
2. Provide leadership and focus. Take responsibility.
3. Communicate clearly and thoroughly with everyone involved.
4. Sell the benefits of working on your team and reinforce them often.
5. Involve team members with customers and prospects and give them responsibility.
6. Value the team's input, praise them and recognise their achievements.
7. Stimulate enthusiasm and have fun.
8. Be firm and decisive if anyone fails – the customer comes first.

In some circumstances, especially if the deal you are working on is large or particularly important, it may be appropriate to expand your team to include senior management. In some deals where the decision-making process goes right to the top of the organisation it can make a lot of sense to have a customer's Chief Executive talk to your Managing Director,

or their Financial Director talk to your Financial Director –
especially if a particularly long-term relationship is envisaged
or if the deal is very high profile for both companies. Such
an approach is sometimes called multi-level selling and, put
simply, you are matching the various levels of your customer's organisation with a similar level from your own to
enable peer to peer discussions. This helps to speed up
communications and fosters better relationships at all levels.
However, if such a team is justified in a sales situation, *never*
forget that *you* are the sales person and that *you* have
complete control of and responsibility for the whole sales
campaign. Many senior managers fancy themselves as sales
people and can become 'loose cannons' if they are not
briefed and managed correctly in advance. It is important that
everyone involved in your team knows exactly what you are
trying to achieve and what role you expect them to play. Do
not be tempted to assume that, because your Managing
Director is involved, you are suddenly of less importance or
that responsibility for success now rests with him. It is your
deal and he is a member of your team. You ultimately call
the shots.

Selling psychologically
Undoubtedly, psychology does come into selling. If we
know what someone is thinking, it makes the process of
selling to him so much easier and effective. Fortunately, it is
possible to understand what is going on in a customer's
mind, both at a general and a specific level, by observing a
few simple principles. I have already touched on the fact that
selling is all about trust and that people often buy things
emotionally. Taking the time to build a relationship, treating
customers uniquely, building rapport, developing trust and
respect, making customers feel important and valued are all
part of this psychological approach. However, it can be
developed further:

1. Body language

Body language was the hot topic in selling a few years ago. Today, it has become another, if quite significant, tool in the salesman's kit bag. Put simply, 'body language' is all about recognising people's mood, temperament or feelings from the physical signs they demonstrate. It is a useful tool because, at times, what people are really thinking or feeling is at odds with what they are saying and this can often be given away by what they reveal physically. However, don't forget that your own body language will also give away what you think or feel too! This topic is too specialised to cover in detail here, but some basic ideas are worth mentioning:

- Eye Contact – keeping eye contact implies an interest in the person you are talking to and that you are listening closely. Eye contact is not about staring, that could be construed as aggressive, and glancing away or looking down to take notes is perfectly acceptable. But making sure that eyes meet occasionally and that you demonstrate you are listening with nods of under- standing, or perhaps a smile, helps to develop a closer relationship.
- Posture – perhaps the classic body language principle. Folded arms can mean a defensive or reserved state of mind. Leaning forward slightly can imply interest. Sitting back in a chair in a relaxed manner, but still talking with animation and maintaining eye contact, implies comfort and enthusiasm.
- Distance and contact – another classic idea is that of the handshake. Many people claim to be able to 'read' a person's character from their handshake, although it is notoriously unreliable. What is more important is that shaking hands is often the closest we ever get, physically, to our customers. Personal space is very important, and crowding people, touching

them inappropriately or standing behind them will make them feel uncomfortable.

2. Names

People like it if you use their names. Apart from the common courtesy, it helps to emphasise your friendliness and interest in them. Failure to remember someone's name can indicate that you do not really care about him and it can undermine the relaxed and sincere approach that you might otherwise have made. Think how you feel if someone gets your name wrong, or even forgets it altogether, and resolve not to make the same mistake. Remembering names can be a problem for some people – me especially – and if you are introduced to a number of people at the same time, it is virtually impossible to remember everyone. Handing out business cards helps, but don't be afraid to write names down and ask anyone to repeat his name if you didn't catch it first time, especially if it is unusual and you need to confirm the spelling. Don't be embarrassed by this. It is part of being professional and most people will welcome the fact that you are interested enough to get their name right.

3. Receiving information

Some research has been done into how people prefer to receive information, especially in how it relates to building up trust and developing relationships. People's preferred style of receiving information falls into one of three main categories: those who receive information visually, those who tend to hear things first and foremost, and those who feel things. There is a body of evidence to show that your selling techniques can be made more effective if you tailor your approach to the individual's preferred way of receiving information. People will trust you more if they feel comfortable with you, which means selling to their particular style. Those who receive information visually tend to say, ''I see what you mean'', or, ''That looks good''. Those who hear things say, ''I hear what you say'', or, ''That sounds good''. And those who feel things say, ''My gut reaction is good'', or, ''I've got a good feeling about that''. Selling to each group is then a matter of adapting your technique to whichever type of person you are dealing with. This may sound contrived, but the evidence appears to show it can work and anything that gives you an edge in closing an order has got to be worth considering.

4. Your own instincts

As human beings, we have a number of senses over and above the five basic ones we all know about. Intuition, gut reactions, perspicacity, educated guessing – all of these can have a bearing in a sales situation. I know some sales managers who pooh-pooh such instincts, claiming they do not exist and that only the tried, tested and demonstrable are of value. This may be true, but I have noticed that, as sales people become more experienced and successful, they do sometimes get 'feelings' about things, feelings which can be relied upon in the absence of hard facts. I am not suggesting that you should base a whole sales campaign on the flimsy belief that you will win just because you feel you should. There is a lot of wishful thinking in selling and it has no place in professional selling. But, just occasionally, a sales person may get a feeling that, although the facts say one thing, his instincts say another and it is always worth just checking things out. In those situations where hard facts are conspicuous by their absence, a gut feeling might be all you have to go on.

The psychology of selling is a complex, often contentious area of research and I have a tendency to see it as academic rather than practical – too many doctors and professors and not enough real sales people involved. However, such a jaundiced view is probably unfair. Just a few years ago, the study of Body Language would have seemed somewhat far-fetched and yet today it is a commonly understood principle. There is a considerable body of literature on the psychology of selling and I would encourage you to investigate the matter further because any tip or technique that improves your effectiveness is worthwhile. It is probably also worth saying that you shouldn't dismiss things out of hand without trying them – and trying them with an open mind rather than half-heartedly or cynically.

7

ENJOYMENT, ATTITUDE AND MONEY

What is enjoyment?

Enjoyment is all about having the enthusiasm to get on and do your job, regardless of the challenges ahead or disappointments of the past; about liking what you do, warts and all. The satisfaction of a job well done can be a reward in itself, but the excitement of a well-fought sales campaign and the pleasure of lifting the order at the end of it are experiences that the successful sales person is keen to repeat again and again. Enjoyment is contagious – if customers enjoy doing business with you they are likely to come back for more, and colleagues will welcome the chance to work with you again. From a psychological point of view, enjoyment reinforces optimism and optimism is one of the key attributes of the professional sales person, determining how motivated he can be and how well he can bounce back from setbacks.

The right attitude

You often hear the phrase 'Positive Mental Attitude' used as a desirable characteristic for sales people. The phrase stems from the 'motivational industry' that started in America in the 1950s and it has moved into general usage, denoting a focused and dynamic 'go getter'. Frankly, the phrase scares me to death! All too often a Positive Mental Attitude implies an almost arrogant confidence which I think is at odds with being a professional sales person. Nobody likes pushy, overbearing, aggressively confident people and it's a fair bet that your customers will be put off by such an attitude. That is not to say that sales people need to be meek and mild though. Great sales people really are positive and dynamic individuals – go-getters in the very real sense that they bring in more and better business than anyone else – but this stems from an unshakable belief that they hold the ability to achieve success in their own hands, rather than an arrogant assumption that success is theirs by right.

The way you think about your job is one of the most powerful influences on how well you can do it. Your attitude determines not only how much success you can achieve but also the sort of impression you will make on your customers when you meet them. Your character is made up of a multitude of different attributes and it determines how you view life in general, as well the abilities that you can bring to bear on your job. The following characteristics are shared by all top sales people:

1. Optimism

Optimism is the true expression of a positive outlook on life. It is an approach that confronts any setback with the quiet confidence that things are, or will be, better than they seem. A pessimistic frame of mind can only generate a negative outcome or response: constantly being critical without foreseeing any constructive way forward, or moaning and complaining all the time, are bound to make you and your associates unhappy. By constantly working to emphasise the positive in every situation, we reinforce optimism and confidence. By practising optimism we reinforce its influence on every aspect of our lives. By believing that for every problem there really is an answer, we will have more energy to tackle the challenges that confront us. By knowing in advance that things will improve, things will have already started to get better.

2. Confidence

You are the only person who can make your success happen and if you do not believe in yourself no-one else will. Belief in yourself is not arrogance and confidence is largely the result of familiarity with, rather than an overbearing belief in, your abilities. Confidence comes from knowing what you are doing. We tend to lack confidence when we have to start something new or when we are unsure of what to do and what the outcome might be. Fear of the consequences stops people from trying anything new or challenging. Yet, when you stop to think about it, what would be the worst thing that could happen if you did try something new? Embarrassment, disapproval, a sense of failure, being told off, anger? Well, so what? You can live with all of these. It is the fear of what might happen that stops most people from succeeding and not the thing itself. *We* contribute to our lack of confidence, not the reactions of other people. Confidence is a habit that can be reinforced by practice and preparation. Do the groundwork and leave as little to chance as possible.

3. Desire

Being successful is hard work. It takes planning and effort, perspiration and ability. But success will continue to be elusive if you do not also desire it. Passion is not normally a word associated with selling, but when it comes to being the best, having a passion for what you do is essential. You can succeed at anything you want if you believe with every fibre of your being that you will achieve it. Top sales people are driven to achieve success. They are not content with second best. They have to win. And this desire – this passion to succeed – gives them the strength and determination to go that extra mile in order to achieve it. It is desire, not ability, that determines success.

4. Motivation

Sales people work in an ever-changing environment and are stimulated and intrigued by the new, the unexpected or the challenging. They are also driven to win and their motivation comes from this need to succeed. The material trappings – especially money – are desirable, but they are as much a measure of success as a goal in themselves. Motivation means that instead of being defeated by problems, sales people are driven to find a way around them. Challenges are there to be overcome because any barrier to success stimulates the competitive instinct and sales people will employ all of the powers at their command – intelligence, creativity, persistence and experience – to get where they want to be. Success, and the rewards that go with it, are all the motivation they need to tackle the next challenge and the next.

5. Persistence

Persistence is all about stamina; about having the strength of character never to take 'no' for an answer; never to accept the game as lost until it is won. Successful sales people know that the more you attempt the more you will succeed. They put all of their effort into everything they try because they know that, even if they don't succeed, they can learn something of value from the effort, which will help them get further next time.

6. Enthusiasm

Work is a part of just about everybody's lives and it accounts for a good third of all our time. It is vital that, no matter what we do to earn a living, we enjoy it. Selling can be one of the most enjoyable and rewarding careers there is. However, selling is also a demanding profession and, no matter how much we enjoy the job, it isn't going to be enjoyable all the time. The ability to find enthusiasm to do the job, even in the most demanding of situations, is something all successful sales people share. Just doing it for the money is a recipe for disaster. Money may be important, and for most it is a prime motivator, but if it is the only reason you do the job, you are unlikely to be able to continue long-term. As the cliché has it: 'Money can't buy happiness' and, if you are not happy doing what you do, you will become cynical, depressed, burnt-out or disillusioned. You have to like what you do in order to be truly good at it, otherwise you will never put your heart and soul into it. And total commitment is the key to success.

7. Responsibility
Look at the people in the world who make things happen, who are respected and who are successful. Who are they? They are the people who take responsibility, make decisions and then make sure those decisions are carried out. There are few things more infuriating than people who will not take responsibility for their actions or who are incapable of making decisions. Top professionals take responsibility for their own success and they do not blame others for their failures. They know that their success rests in their own hands and does not depend on other people. To base your success on that of other people, or to make others accountable for your actions, is to lose control. Real success can only come if you make decisions for yourself and see things through to their conclusion, taking responsibility for the whole process. Anything less is unprofessional.

The rewards
All sales people are motivated by money to some extent, but there is more to a remuneration package than just cash. I have detailed below a number of items which I have seen included in a sales person's package, for reference purposes. It may not

be exhaustive, but a good package will include many of these in one form or another:

Basic salary

Commission/Bonus

A guarantee against commission, or the opportunity to draw some commission in advance during your induction period

Joining bonus/golden hand-cuffs

Pension scheme – either a company scheme, a private option or a cash allowance

Fully expensed company car or a cash allowance sufficient to fund your own vehicle

Fuel card, petrol allowance or mileage allowance

Health Insurance – individually or for your family, or a cash allowance

Life insurance – a company scheme or a cash allowance

Share save schemes – usually long-term schemes

Share options – often an enticement in new companies, if a bit of a gamble

Membership of sports/health clubs

Discounts on company products

Laptop/Computer

Mobile phone/pager

Facilities to work from home

Out of pocket expenses for entertaining, subsistence, travel and accommodation

Relocation allowances – if you have to move to take up a position

Holidays – in addition to statutory holidays, with additional days for long service

The best salaries and commissions tend to be in either the emerging, potentially more risky, industries like information technology, e-commerce and software sales, or in those where the value of the goods is large and the timescales for completing a deal are long, as in aircraft sales or mainframe computers. However, although salary and commission are the most important elements in any package, the other items can also be significant. For example, your main employment concern might be security, so a slightly less well-paid position with an established company might be particularly attractive because the rest of the remuneration package – quality car, health insurance for the whole family and an excellent pension scheme – offsets the lower basic salary.

In virtually all sales positions your remuneration will comprise two elements – a fixed element (the basic salary) and a variable element (the commission or bonus – sometimes the variable element is capped so that, no matter how much you sell you will never earn more than a certain amount of commission). This is the area where a sales person gets a large percentage of his motivation from. He can see that, if he does his job well and exceeds his targets, he will earn significant amounts of additional money, over and above his basic salary. It is entirely up to him how far he takes this, but the opportunity to earn as much as he wants is there within his own hands. There is a direct relationship between his hard work and the amount he can earn and for most of us this is a major motivating factor.

At the risk of dampening things down a little, it is worth mentioning here that some companies do have a habit of changing the commission structure or moving the goal posts every now and again and it can be a major bone of contention for some sales people, especially if they thought they would earn 'x' for closing a particular deal and find they only get paid 'y'. Such companies don't usually retain good sales people for long, but, no matter who you work for, it is in your best interests that you understand exactly how the commission scheme works, including any small print. For example, in the computer industry, commission tends to be paid in two stages:

50% when an order is booked and the remaining 50% when the equipment is installed and signed off by the customer. Much time can pass between these two events!

Most commission schemes contain a phrase like ''The Sales Director's decision is final'', which sometimes gives you a chance to appeal if you think you are hard done by, but don't gain a reputation for being difficult by abusing it. A disagreement over commission is probably less important than losing your job.

When talking about remuneration, it is also worthwhile just touching on tax. In the euphoria of bringing in a big deal and banking a big commission cheque, it is easy to overlook the fact that the taxman will have an interest in what you are earning. When added to your basic salary, commission can easily push you into a higher tax bracket and all the additional perks, like company cars, petrol allowances and health insurance are seen as taxable too. Tax can seem boring, and it can definitely be complex, but it is in your best interests to know exactly what you should be paying. Mistakes can and will be made at times but no-one else will be concerned unless you are.

Sales awards

Many companies offer a range of sales incentives, over and above the commission and bonus schemes, to motivate people to over-achieve and to reward top performers. These can range from simple cash incentives to all-singing, all-dancing Club Trips, where the top salesmen are whisked away to some exotic location for a few days pampering. To reach the 'top performers club' can be a real badge of success and a major incentive for a lot of sales people – you are acknowledged by your peers to be the best – but cash incentives are also a major motivator for many. These can take any number of forms, for example: increasing the commission rate on those products and services the company is especially keen to push (usually the hardest ones to sell!); offering a bonus on sales made early on in the year because early revenues are good for the bottom

line; commission multipliers for people who exceed their
targets, either monthly, quarterly or yearly; extra bonuses if
discounts are kept within agreed limits (or reduced bonuses or
penalties if such limits are exceeded) and bonuses for getting
payments in early or for cash with order.

Top salesmen are whisked away to some exotic location for a few days
pampering.

Some companies like to reward team performances, especially if technical support, clerical staff and other team members have been instrumental in a particular success and would
not normally get any recognition. I have driven racing cars at
F1 circuits, been powerboating in luxury sea-cruisers, spent
weekends away on activity events quad-biking and clay
pigeon shooting, and received no end of Christmas hampers,
gifts and discount vouchers. All because 'my' team did particularly well. Any company I have worked for where a
regular sales league has been published so that everyone can

see how well they are doing (or not) has enjoyed improved motivation and incentive to do better. Those at the bottom are embarrassed to be there and try to do better, and those at the top want to stay up there. All of this is an immense amount of fun and adds to the enjoyment of a sales career. It increases the competitive spirit to the advantage of everyone while generally improving teamwork and motivation.

Looking after yourself

No matter how motivated or successful the sales person, there are external influences that can affect his long term enjoyment of what he does. Selling is a means to an end, not an end in itself, and if you cannot enjoy the fruits of your labours because of ill-health, stress, or poor personal relationships, even the most enjoyable job will suffer. Enjoyment means looking after yourself physically and mentally; after all, if you are not up to the job, how can you expect to do it well? I know dozens of sales people who do not look after themselves. They slump in front of computers, get trapped in their cars for hours, find they don't have time to eat properly, smoke too much, drink too much coffee and alcohol, and generally treat their bodies with little regard. It may not appear to affect their ability to do the job properly, but I have noticed that a significant proportion suffer from longer term health problems which, even if not life threatening, degrade their quality of life.

I am not about to lecture you on the merits of leading a healthy life, but, as we spend a good third of our lives working, it helps if we enjoy our jobs as much as possible. If we feel 'under the weather', 'stressed out' or suffer from recurring health problems, our ability to enjoy what we do will be compromised. And our ability to perform properly might be affected too. If you have to take time off work on a regular basis because a health problem keeps flaring up or because you keep catching every bug going, your career is in danger of being affected and you will have little control over your accounts and territory. Many of us put up with or ignore health problems, hoping they will just go away, but this is a poor investment strategy. Investing in good health reaps dividends in increased vitality, longevity, mental sharpness and the ability to enjoy what we do. With many jobs offering free private medical cover or health insurance, as well as membership of health clubs, there is no excuse for not being fit and well. There is also plenty of free advice and guidance around and I have detailed eight basic rules for good health below, which apply to all sales people:

1.   If you smoke, try and give up. Smoking is the main cause of premature death. Heart disease, cancers, premature aging of the skin, bones and lungs – all are the direct result of smoking.

2.   Drink alcohol in moderation. Aim for at least two alcohol free days a week and, if you are driving, do not drink alcohol at all. These days I find that most customers require much less wining and dining than in the past and, even when you do have to entertain, there is wide acceptance that a glass of water or a soft drink is a sensible choice. Your whole career will be jeopardised if you get arrested for driving under the influence of alcohol.

3.   Exercise regularly. Find an activity that you enjoy which makes you breathless and makes you sweat and which you can do at least three times a week for a minimum of twenty minutes a time. Exercise is not just an essential part of good health, it is also one of the most effective ways of alleviating stress. The sheer pleasure and effort of exerting the body, of making yourself physically tired, is often the best antidote to a difficult day at work.

4.   Eat healthily. Include plenty of cereals, fresh fruit and vegetables in your diet and go easy on the cream, butter, fatty foods, sugar and cakes. If you like a fry up at a 'greasy spoon' while out on the road (I know I do) try

not to indulge every day. Choose a healthier option off
the menu when entertaining clients.

5.   Watch your weight. We tend to sit around a lot as sales
     people, either in the office or in the car, and most of the
     older among us would admit to a little 'middle-aged
     spread'. If you find your belt is getting too tight, do
     something about it. It will improve your appearance and
     your self-image, as well as your health.

6.   Have regular medical check-ups. Screening tests can
     detect many diseases before they cause illness and while
     treatment is still easy. Get treatment for any nagging or
     recurring health complaints.

7.   Don't get into the habit of taking work home with you. It
     may occasionally be unavoidable, but your family and
     friends won't thank you for it and we all need to be able
     to switch off at times.

8.   Develop or maintain outside interests. There is nothing
     so dull or wearing as someone who talks about work all
     the time. And if all you can think about is work, you
     stand the chance of mental burn-out. Small talk is an
     important part of establishing rapport with customers in
     certain circumstances and it will be all the harder if you
     have nothing to say.

Health – a personal view

For a long time I put up with a back problem which made
driving long distances very uncomfortable. I kept putting off
going to the doctor thinking it would sort itself out, but it
didn't. It got worse and I found myself trying to avoid
appointments that involved lots of driving, which started to
have an impact on my sales figures. At the back of my mind I
think I knew the problem would only be sorted out with rest,
but I told myself that I couldn't afford the time and I soldiered
on, putting up with the pain and my disappointing sales
performance as best I could. Ironically, the solution came

when I damaged my leg playing five-a-side football. The back problem was making me increasingly less nimble and I failed to get out of the way of a particularly robust tackle. I told the specialist about my back problem when she decided to put my leg in a plaster cast and she diagnosed a torn muscle in the small of my back – something that was exacerbated by long periods of sitting. The treatment for both the leg and the back was rest and to lie down as much as possible. I went through a period of anxiety about not being able to service my accounts properly, but this quickly gave way to an acceptance that there was nothing I could do about it with my leg in a cast, and I could still use the phone whenever necessary. Subsequently, I have never had a recurrence of the problem and my sales figures improved as driving stopped being (literally) a pain.

Managing stress
Selling is an inherently stressful profession. It is competitive, thrives on action, drives itself hard and is always in a hurry – the very characteristics which attracted us to the job in the first place. It is basically a people business, which means it can be unpredictable and sometimes emotional. We have to work to targets and deadlines and we have a lot of personal responsibility. Sometimes, large sums of money can be involved too. All of this has a pressure-cooker effect that can be hard to avoid. You can become anxious about all the things you have to complete, worry about whether you can do everything, fret about those who may be let down, torture yourself with fear about the personal consequences of failing to complete certain key actions and ultimately waste time worrying about doing everything without starting to do anything at all. The pressure builds up until you become 'stressed out' – literally unable to function properly because worry and fear paralyse your ability to act. This type of situation feeds on itself, eating into the time available to you so that you are always trying to catch up rather than being in control.

The professional sales person has to learn to manage the pressures of the job and, when things are going well and you can enjoy what you are doing, stress is unlikely to be a problem. But, if things aren't going so well, pressure can start to build up and problems can seem increasingly insurmountable. Here are some tips to help you work through such periods – we all get them occasionally:

1. Most people are at their most productive and effective in the morning. Use this time for your most important work. If you prioritise your workload and draw up a list of the things you need to do during the day, make sure you physically cross each item off the list as it is completed – you can see your workload diminishing, along with any stress associated with it. Delegate or reject anything that is not your immediate responsibility.

2. Talk to people. A lack of information is often the root cause of stress and if you feel that you are being kept in the dark or have insufficient information to do your job as you would like, irritations and dissatisfaction will develop. Sales people are by nature self-sufficient and resilient. It can be difficult to ask for help or advice, but with some problems two heads are better than one. Don't listen to rumours, gossip, half-truths and innuendo.

3. Don't worry. Worry saps your ability to act and feeds on itself, dragging you deeper into despair and inaction. There are only two types of problems that cause worry – those you can do something about and those that you can't. With those you can do nothing about, accept the consequences and get prepared to deal with the results. If there is something you can do, get on and do it. You will break the cycle of despair and start to see things improve. For example, if your car breaks down, getting angry over missing an appointment and worrying about the knock-on effects is totally pointless. If you have a mobile

phone, get on and tell everyone what has happened. If you haven't, get a piece of paper and plan what you will do when the problem is sorted out. Chain-smoking, drumming your fingers on the steering wheel, leaping in and out of the car, pacing up and down, and wishing the problem hadn't happened at such a critical time, will only wind you up without achieving anything.

4. Don't allow current pressures and problems to cause your mind to dredge up past wrongs, injustices, failures, disappointments and setbacks. You are unlikely to be able to deal with the current problem properly if your mind keeps dwelling on how bad things always seem to be for you. Fate doesn't have it in for you and you alone – the arrogance of feeling you are that important will hinder any chance of success. Only look back into the past if there is a solution there you can use to resolve present problems.

5. Try not to get angry. Anger is a natural response to pressure and can be entirely justified in certain circumstances, but we rarely get the chance to let it out of our systems so it sits there feeding on itself as it adds to the pressure we feel under. It colours our judgment and can cause us to act irrationally. *You will always regret anything said or done when angry*. Walk away. Count to ten. Go to the driving range and take it out on a few dozen golf balls. And then come back and deal with things calmly and rationally. The situation will almost certainly be addressable once the red mist fades.

6. Make sure you maintain an active social life. Take up or maintain hobbies that take your mind off work. Take regular physical exercise. Leave work at the office and learn to relax and enjoy yourself at home. You will be able to face your problems refreshed and invigorated and, who knows, they might be just that little bit less daunting once you come to revisit them.

7.   Don't forget to laugh – at yourself, at the ridiculous situations that life sometimes throws at you, at your own fears and apprehensions and at the problems you are faced with. Humour is a great healer and it is very difficult for stress to take hold of you if you are enjoying yourself. Stress can cloud the mind to such an extent that this simple fact can be forgotten or lost amongst the pressure. We can take ourselves and our problems too seriously. By remembering to laugh, you will find relief for your problems. It has been clinically proven that laughter acts as a pressure release valve that helps stress to drain away and it can be the most effective antidote to worry, anxiety, inhibition, doubt and fear.

8

INTEGRITY

What is integrity?
Integrity is the most fundamental attribute of the professional sales person. It determines not only the standards we set for ourselves, but also how we conduct our relationships with others, how we tackle challenges and overcome problems, and how we present ourselves to the world. Integrity inspires confidence and is what others will judge us by – whether we can be relied upon and trusted. Integrity means: 'wholeness, entirety, soundness, uprightness, honesty' (OED). It implies self-discipline and an ability to see things through, as well as a desire to provide the very best service possible. It means taking responsibility for everything we do and say and being accountable for our actions. There is no room for lying or dishonesty in professional selling, nor for unethical behaviour – sloping your shoulder to others, passing the buck, hiding from problems and failing to see things through are the preserve of the weak and unprofessional.

Integrity is also about the long term. Trust is not a tick in the box that once earned remains fixed for ever. Dependability and reliability have to be demonstrated on an ongoing basis if you want to be rewarded with loyalty. Today, the customer's view of you and your company is very often only as good as the last contact made or the weakest link encountered. Customers are no longer as forgiving as they used to be and, with so much choice available to them, unless the service they receive is all they desire, they will be off. The first you will know of it is a cessation of orders. Increasingly, customers don't bother to complain – they just switch suppliers.

What does integrity mean for the professional?

Trust is the basis of all long term relationships and it can be destroyed instantly if your promises and recommendations are founded on lies and deceit. Cynical exploitation purely for financial gain may win you business, but it won't win you loyal customers. Nor will it bring you respect. And a poor reputation will come to haunt you in more ways than one:

- You will always have to start from scratch to find new business rather than developing repeat business from existing customers.
- Deliver shoddy goods or services, or fail to keep your word, and you will end up having to deal with more complaints and irate customers than you can cope with. You may try and avoid them, but your company won't be able to.
- If your whole approach is lax, cynical and untrust-worthy, your chances of keeping a job will be severely reduced. And getting a new one will become increasingly difficult.

Trust means being impartial, objective and honest – not just with your customers, but with your colleagues and associates too. It also means doing what you say you will do and not making rash promises you cannot keep. Customers, in my experience, would rather know up front about problems, the 'hidden' extras and what options they have, rather than be surprised by them later on. They will trust you all the more if you admit to not knowing something and commit to find out (and then do so), rather than trying to invent things or dodging the issue altogether. Telling the truth may not always appear easy, especially if you feel the information is unpalatable, but trying to sustain a lie is even more uncomfortable. Especially as the truth starts to emerge! I am not suggesting that you should wear your heart on your sleeve or give away important secrets or competitive advantage willy-nilly. You have to be selective in what information you reveal during the sales process and tailor it to the individual. But whatever you tell the customer must be true. And whatever you decide to keep to yourself must not be to the customer's detriment, or to yours, should he find out!

Pricing is usually one area where many sales people are tempted to be economical with the truth. They are worried that the customer will say the price is too high or unacceptable and will reject them. The reality is that customers will always query the price, but they do expect you to make a profit because they need you to stay in business if they are going to purchase something from you. And they certainly won't buy anything until they know the price – and the full price at that. Hide the compulsory extras in an attempt to make the price more attractive and you are storing up trouble for yourself, if not a cancelled order, later on.

Be true to yourself
Integrity also means being honest with yourself, even at the expense of looking for another job.

1.   In order to be successful, a sales person needs to be enthusiastic about what he is selling and the company he works for. Without enthusiasm, he will be unable to stimulate desire for his products and services and the effort required to keep on selling in such a situation will grind him down. In the interests of his company,

his customers and himself, any sales person in such a
situation would be advised to find another position
elsewhere.

2.   If the company he works for treats him or his customers
     unfairly, if they do not uphold the values and principles
     that are important to him, then continuing to sell their
     products and services will mean that he is not only
     being dishonest to his customers, but also to himself.
     Again, he needs to seek alternative employment.

3.   If the company he works for does not share his belief in
     excellent customer service or ethical behaviour, prefer-
     ring to rip the customers off, or ignore their justified
     complaints (whether through incompetence or design),
     he must not allow his own reputation to become tainted
     and must leave.

Customer delight

I bet you have very rarely experienced truly excellent customer service. And when you have done, weren't you
delighted – and surprised? Your customers feel exactly the
same way. Excellent service does not begin once the customer
takes delivery of his purchase. It is an ongoing process that
starts at your very first contact with a prospect, continues
through to the delivery of a product or service that at least
meets, if not exceeds, expectations, and then develops further
as a long term relationship is established.

Customer service is quite rightly seen as the most important 'value added' element in the marketplace, but all too
many companies provide 'lip service' rather than something
concrete and tangible – a marketing gloss instead of a
genuine desire to please the customer. After all, good
customer service takes effort, money and long term vision
and these are often difficult for the short-sighted to sustain.
Yet, excellent customer service pays for itself in terms of
repeat business, customer retention, market awareness,

reputation and references. Top sales people understand this. They know that as owners of the initial relationship with the customer, they (personally) are the 'value added' ingredient in the sales process. They know that if customers are delighted not only with the product or service they receive, but also with the whole sales and delivery process, they will keep on coming back for more. And will tell others to do the same.

In the modern business environment, the sales person is unlikely to be personally responsible for delivering his product or service. Commodity products are manufactured, delivered and invoiced by faceless production and delivery facilities, while more complex solutions are implemented by specific implementation teams, with back up from customer service centres and after sales support staff. No matter how good any of these facilities is, it is inevitable that, with so many different people involved, something might go wrong at some stage. It is also unlikely that anyone other than the sales person will care quite so much about delivery. After all, the others don't know the customer as well, and haven't developed the trust and relationship. This is not to imply that no-one else cares about customer service; of course, many people do. But the sales person owns the initial relationship with the customer. He knows what was promised and what the customer expects and, if he does not manage the whole process of delivery in some way, there is a chance that the customer will be disappointed at some stage. Also, if he knows what is going on, when a problem does crop up, he can cover it with the customer immediately.

With this in mind, the best professionals introduce key individuals to the customer early on in the sales cycle. Not only does it show a depth of resource and a company-wide interest in customer service, it helps relationships and understanding to develop long before the actual offering has to be delivered.

1. Introduce project managers, customer service and technical support staff early on in the sales cycle so that strong relationships can be developed. Their input can sometimes help to close a sale early because the customer is confident about the delivery process.

2. Introduce billing and financial personnel so that account queries can be handled by someone the customer knows, rather than a faceless individual.

3. Make sure that all legal, financial, billing, delivery and implementation details are fully understood, entered on the right systems (with the correct names and addresses) and that the customer's specific requirements are understood and met.

4. Ensure delivery times are realistic and that both parties agree on what is reasonable. Agree contingencies and back-up if there is any likelihood of slippage.

5. Provide the customer with all the contact names and numbers he will require in order to maintain adequate contact with your company. Always make yourself available as necessary.

6. Ensure that, if any form of professional service is required (training, consultancy, or implementation services), the customer is aware of it and your staff are well briefed, introduced early and that both parties understand the scope of work required.

7. Maintain contact with the customer to ensure he is happy with everything at all times.

8. Try phoning your own company anonymously some time and see what sort of service you get. It is a good way of gauging what sort of response your own customers and prospects might receive and it can sometimes be something of a shock.

9. In many instances, especially in the case of new customers or particularly large or important deals, the company might appoint an executive sponsor to monitor

delivery. The sales person must liaise with him on an regular basis.

I know a lot of sales people who don't do these things and who are then surprised when they have to manage complaints and sort out all manner of problems. Most companies do not want their sales people getting involved in delivery issues because they want them out selling. If you want to avoid getting sucked back in to sort out problems, then it is vital to ensure the delivery team understands in detail exactly what the customer wants, and has some ownership of the customer relationship. The sales person develops the relationship with the customer and, if he is going to sell him more in the future, that relationship must continue to be strong. And that can only happen if the customer is happy with the total service he receives.

Remember:

1. Customers are important – without them your company will disappear because they provide the ongoing revenue and profits for the business.
2. Customers may not always know what they want, but they do know what they don't want and that is poor service. Today they don't always complain because they can get up and go elsewhere so easily.
3. Customer expectations only go one way – up. Trust and loyalty have to be earned on an ongoing basis otherwise you run the risk of disappointment and dissatisfaction, which will lead to defection.
4. Successful sales people get close to their customers, taking the time to understand their needs, wants and expectations and then ensure these are understood by their company and met.
5. Successful sales people don't make promises to customers they can't keep and they manage customer expectations to avoid disappointment.

Setting expectations

Setting expectations is a vital procedure if you want to avoid disputes or recriminations later on in the sales process. It may seem obvious to you what is and what is not included in the price and specification of your offering, but it may not be to your customer. If you don't check his understanding, the customer may well be expecting rather more than is being delivered and you will have to manage his disappointment or disagreement. This is as true for commodity sales as it is for large, complex solutions where there are more variables to consider. For example: the 'batteries not included' warning on children's electric toys and the like helps to set the purchasers' expectation that they will also have to buy batteries in order to make the toy work. Without it (and this has happened to all of us) your child unpacks his present on Christmas Day only to be totally disappointed because there are no batteries included and he cannot play with it. It usually means he will continue to be disappointed with the toy too, even when you do get the batteries, and it is quite likely to gather dust in a corner. Customers often feel the same. If their initial expectations are not met, no amount of appeasement or reconciliation can offset their feeling of being let down.

Telling a customer what to expect isn't just the honest approach, it is common sense, but that doesn't mean that all sales people practise it. Through fear or worry they sometimes try to avoid difficult issues – again, often because they are concerned that, for example an admission of how little is included in the base price will lose them the sale, or that a particularly long delivery time might put the customer off. This is short sighted and, if a customer is under the impression that the price includes (in the case of a car, say) leather upholstery, or that he can take delivery within a week, finding out that leather is actually an optional extra which he hasn't paid for or that delivery is really two months away, will come as a serious blow. And he'll be even more unhappy if the sales person smugly pulls out the contract and shows him the small print saying leather is a costed option he hasn't paid for. If the customer doesn't cancel the order then and there the sales person will be very lucky, but his reputation will be sullied forever in the eyes of the customer.

It is in everybody's best interest to get everything out in the open and to understand exactly what the customer will get for his money and what he won't. That way there can be no argument and the customer will trust you more. Also, by doing so early on in a sale, a sales person gains a good opportunity to sell the add-ons and upgrades that might make a small sale a much larger one. In solutions selling where a complex, bespoke offering is constructed for the customer, making sure both parties agree on what is and isn't included becomes very important. Some elements can become negotiating items and the sales person might chose to 'lose' some consultancy services here or a piece of software there in order to close a particularly large deal. This can often help to avoid discounting prices for the main elements of the order, but it can only work if the customer understands that such 'freebies' are essential to the overall solution and that they would normally have to pay for them.

Service Level Agreements
Closely associated with setting expectations are Service Level Agreements (SLAs), which are often negotiated and contracted for in the same way as more standard contractual Terms and Conditions. An SLA is a record of exactly what sort of service your company commits to provide to the customer, and it will often contain penalty clauses and payments for non-delivery. The SLA will also detail commitments that the customer must adhere to in order for your company to be able to provide the agreed level of service. For example, a cleaning company secures a contract to clean an office building. They commit to clean the whole building between the

hours of 8.00 pm and 2.00 am every night, five nights a week, to a quality standard agreed by both parties (all floors to be hoovered, all toilets cleaned and restocked with paper, towels, soap etc., all coffee facilities restocked and so on). If the cleaning company fail to achieve this level of service they agree to pay the customer a fee for every point they fail on. However, the customer equally has to commit to ensuring the cleaning staff always have access to the building between 8.00 pm and 2.00 am and that stocks of coffee, soap, towels etc. are available to complete the job properly. Clearly you are unlikely to be negotiating SLAs if you sell tins of beans to corner shops, but the principle of setting expectations about the service behind the product is the same – delivery times, number of deliveries, reorder timescales and so on.

Handling problems

It doesn't often happen, but occasionally you will find that a product or service you have sold turns out to be unreliable or unsuitable. Handling problems is a key skill for sales people and complaints should be welcomed rather than feared or avoided. If something he has sold does not live up to the customer's expectations the professional sales person will want to know about it as soon as possible because he wants to put it right. We have all seen the sign on restaurant walls, "If our service was lousy, tell us. If it was excellent, tell everyone else!", and this applies to the professional sales person. He knows bad news travels fast and wants to avoid it, but more importantly, he wants the chance to correct the problem. His reputation and integrity are at stake and he is genuinely disappointed that his recommendations have failed to materialise as expected.

Here are my suggestions on how to handle complaints or problems as professionally as possible:

1. Be polite and courteous. Don't increase the pressure your customer is already under. Avoid stupid questions. Tell

the truth. Don't make a claim you can't substantiate and don't let your irritations show. Take responsibility. Don't pass the buck or blame others. Do not run your company down either.

2. Listen carefully to the complaint without interrupting. Let him get it all out, especially if he is angry. Apologise if it is appropriate, even if it is for his anxiety. Remain calm. If you react when you have only got half the story then, at best, you can only give a half-hearted response, which might cause more problems than it resolves.

3. Be sympathetic. Reassure the person that you understand his situation and that he has every right to voice his opinions. Do not argue or get irritated, no matter how provoked.

4. Make sure you really do understand the problem and that you have got all of the details right. Accept what he has to say at face value at this stage. Gently ask questions to elicit all of the facts and to encourage the complainant to get it all out. Try to understand why a situation has arisen and do not attempt to make a judgment yet.

5. Once he has run out of steam, tell him you understand his problem by summarising what he has told you. Ask him if you've got it right so that he starts to agree with you. If you have listened properly and can demonstrate that you really do understand his problem or concern, he will feel more confident that you will be able to help and antagonism will drain away. He may even become conciliatory and apologise for any anger he might have shown.

6. Once you understand the problem thoroughly, you will be in a much better position to make a judgment and to decide on what to do next. If the complaint is justified, apologise unreservedly and, if you have it within your

power to resolve the situation, do so as quickly as possible. If not, explain what steps need to be taken and undertake personally to ensure that they are indeed carried out. Agree with the customer that your proposed plan will resolve his complaint.

7.   Once you have outlined a course of action and the customer has agreed that this will resolve the situation, it is **mandatory** to do what you said you would do and to ensure that everything is followed up correctly, even if other people become involved. Keep in touch with the customer to gauge progress. Get this stage right and, far from being resentful, the customer may even be encouraged to feel happy with your response and the continuing good service, which will stand you in good stead when he next comes to order. Whatever you do, do not be tempted to ignore the customer or to hide things under the carpet through fear or embarrassment.

8.   If the complaint is unjustified, apologise for the confusion. Do not take offence. Blame yourself if necessary for being unclear and then politely and calmly go through things thoroughly so that he can see a mistake hasn't been made. Give the complainer a chance to 'save face' if appropriate – if he can see he has been at fault or is complaining unnecessarily he will be embarrassed or apologetic. Handle things with good grace and dismiss it as inconsequential. Do not be tempted to drag it up again in the future.

9.   In some circumstances, the sales person will find out that there is a problem before the customer complains or becomes aware of the issue. It is essential to sort out a remedy immediately and then contact the customer to tell him not only that there is a problem, but also to advise him of the resolution and how long it will take. If you are upfront about the problem and demonstrate that it is under control in this way, the customer is much more

likely to be able to handle the situation – after all he hadn't spotted the problem and so it hasn't become an issue for him yet. He may be irritated that something hasn't gone as smoothly as expected, but he will certainly appreciate the honesty and quick response demonstrated by your company, and this can only be good for long term relationships.

9

TRAINING

What is training?

The dictionary defines training as: "bringing to a desired state or standard of efficiency by instruction or practice". For me, training is all about acquiring practical knowledge and skills in order to enhance your natural talents and so improve your ability to do a particular job.

Training is essential for every sales person, whatever his level of success or ability. It is an investment rather than an overhead. Anyone who feels that he cannot improve his skills just that bit more, who can't afford the time, or who feels he knows it all already, is dead in the water. His opposition (and even his customers) will be taking advantage of anything that can improve their effectiveness and the complacent sales person will very quickly be overtaken in the race for success. Sportsmen or soldiers would never think of taking to the field without practising their skills, learning to work as a team or becoming proficient with their equipment, and selling is no different. It is just as competitive, tough and unremitting.

Selling is such a natural part of life that it is often taken for granted. But just because you have talent doesn't mean it can't be improved upon or developed further. Raw ability needs moulding and shaping in order to make it as effective as possible, yet sales people are often expected to learn on the job; to have their rough edges smoothed out in the school of hard knocks. Unfortunately, although practice makes perfect, you will only be successful if you practise the right way to do things. And if you aren't shown or don't know the right way, the chances are you will end up reinforcing bad habits and poor technique. Just because someone appears to present themselves well and can talk fluently doesn't mean he will be effective when meeting customers. Yet sales people are sent out every day without anyone checking what they are going to say or whether they understand the role they need to fulfil.

Training helps to develop your talents and to improve any areas of weakness or deficiency. It shows you the right way to do things so that you get off on the right foot, and gives you an opportunity to practise properly without the embarrassment of doing it for real in front of a customer. It doesn't mean you will be word perfect when you visit the next customer, but at least you won't be trying it for the first time. Training also introduces you to the latest techniques and keeps your knowledge up to date. This is essential in today's marketplace. Selling is a constantly evolving profession – what happened to all of those door to door salesmen of the past – and new opportunities like the Internet need to be grasped and understood. Customers are increasingly sophisticated and will know all about closing techniques and negotiating skills. And your competition will be honing their abilities on a continual basis in order to steal your customers. Think I'm exaggerating? Just look at the proliferation of independent training organisations – they are only in business because there is a demand for their services. However, training is ultimately no substitute for doing it for real though it is worth bearing in mind that some people excel in the classroom, but become mediocre out in the field. Training is only part of the story. Once you have had a good grounding in the basics and have had a chance to make your initial mistakes in private, getting out and doing it for real is the only way to become professional.

How to get trained

Selling isn't rocket science and most 'sales techniques' are basically common sense, but a good grounding in common sense doesn't do anyone any harm! Also, with the stakes being so high, making sure you start off on the right foot and keep on track as your career develops is essential to long term success. Most of us, when we think about training, tend to hark back to school and tedious afternoons spent studying algebra when we would rather have been out playing football or swimming. Many sales people dread the thought of being 'locked up' in some conference centre somewhere, discussing closing techniques, or being dragged into some motivational seminar. Luckily, although formal 'classroom' training is important, it isn't the only way to get trained.

1. Learning from colleagues

Observe those sales people who you most admire and look at what they do, how they speak and present themselves, and how they handle customers. A lot of basic sales techniques are absorbed subliminally as you go about your daily business: overhearing phone calls, watching people present at company briefings, discussions with colleagues over coffee or sales team meetings. Obviously, you can pick up bad habits too, but a lot of basic messages are learned in this way, especially about how your particular company goes about doing business. Never be afraid to ask your colleagues or your manager how to do something if you are in doubt.

2. Supplier seminars and conferences

These can be an excellent source of product and market information, as well as a good way of making contacts with people. Most suppliers – your own company included – will hold briefing sessions of some sort for their customers, partners and the wider marketplace. Try and get invitations whenever possible. Exhibitions and conferences are also a good source of information and many suppliers give free briefings or demonstrations which anyone can attend.

3. Distance learning
Many companies now provide self-help training facilities, whether over the Internet, via CDs on a PC, or by video and cassette. Although they are no substitute for human interaction, they can be a very useful addition to on the job learning and you can at least work through the material at your own pace. There is an increasing range of such facilities available, ranging from basic skills like computer literacy up to more complex abilities like time management, negotiating skills and interview techniques.

4. Books and magazines
As with Distance Learning, there is a wealth of published material on selling skills. There are also magazines and periodicals aimed at sales and marketing professionals which are well worth subscribing to. Don't forget that the quality newspapers and business journals also run articles on selling, as well as general business and market details, and these are always a rich source of up to the minute information. It is good practice to subscribe to a quality daily newspaper, especially one with a good business section (e.g. the *Financial Times* or *Wall Street Journal*), as well as periodicals like the *Economist* or *Newsweek*, in order to keep abreast of what is going on in the world in general. There are now a number of on-line journals, newsletters and briefing services available over the Internet, which might also be useful.

5. Company briefings
Your company will almost certainly run seminars and briefing sessions for its staff and these are well worth attending, even if it is just to find out from senior management what the company's strategy and goals are. There are usually new

product launches and briefings too, as well as the company's technical, sales and marketing literature. If the company participates in exhibitions and conferences, make sure you attend in order to find out what is going on in the wider marketplace. If your company has technical or support staff, spend some time with them to increase your product knowledge, as well as to develop a close working relationship with them.

6. Customer training facilities

Many companies, especially if they sell complex products and services, provide training facilities and courses for new customers. If you find you are lacking in any of the areas covered by these courses try and sit in on any customer events being held or get copies of the course material to study on your own. Your colleagues in the training department may also be able to help run through things on an informal basis, especially if you buy them a beer later on!

Nevertheless, formal training sessions are also important and a lot of companies provide induction training for new starters, both in their approved sales techniques, as well as products and services. There are also a wide range of sales training courses available from third party organisations and most businesses will invest in some external training facilities for their sales teams at some time or other. There are several advantages to courses of this sort:

- They get you off site so you are away from the distractions of the office.
- They give you the opportunity to make contact with people from other parts of the organisation who you might not normally come into contact with.
- They enable whole sections of the company to be trained at one time so everyone is 'singing from the same song sheet', as it were, rather than having everyone at different levels of understanding and effectiveness.

- The best courses involve teamwork and foster a competitive edge, which is great for helping morale and developing strong relationships in the workplace.

Whatever your view of such courses, formal training does help to ensure that you get off on the right foot and that you keep on the right path as your career develops. Many sales people, as they get older and more settled in their careers, feel they do not need training. It takes them out of the field and they believe they can ill afford the time. They often feel they know it all anyway. Such complacency is the kiss of death. The marketplace is developing constantly. It doesn't stand still for one minute. If a sales person gets into a comfort zone – a nice set of customers and a standard set of sales skills which see him doing very nicely thank you – it will become a rut that he will eventually be unable to escape from. Keeping up to date is essential for everyone. Anything that can improve your competitive edge has got be of value. Unless you are prepared to change and adapt; to learn new ways of doing things and to address the changes and developments of your marketplace, you will eventually become obsolete.

Unfortunately, no matter how good a sales training course is, nearly all sales people will revert back to previous behaviour as soon as they get back into their cars. Very little taught knowledge sticks if it isn't used and most sales people stick with the tried and tested, even if it isn't terribly effective. Make sure that you keep an open mind and do not approach training with a cynical, 'heard it all before' attitude. If you learn just one thing that makes winning business even 1% more effective, the course will have had a value. Also bear in mind that most companies are very poor at providing training for their staff. Push for it whenever possible and attend when it is available (if nothing else, it looks good on your CV if you are looking for another job!). Make sure you learn things for yourself if formal training is not forthcoming.

Nearly all sales people will revert back to previous behaviour as soon as they get back into their cars.

What sort of training?
The professional sales person needs to be trained in three key areas:

1.   Products and services.
2.   Selling skills.
3.   Business knowledge.

Products and services
In order to sell effectively, you need to know what you are selling inside out. We live in a rapidly developing environment and up to date knowledge is your stock in trade, especially given the speed of change. By and large, training in specific products and services can only come from the company you work for and it is in their best interests to ensure that such training is provided. If it isn't you should request it because, without it, you will be less competitive. The more

technical the offering, the more important the training is.

Such training should also include: an understanding of the company's pricing policy, terms of business, contracts, delivery and production schedules and so on. Customers will ask detailed questions and, while it is acceptable to say ''I'm not sure of the answer to that question. I'll find out and get back to you'', you can only get away with it once or twice before you start to look a bit foolish. In training a sales force in products and services it helps if some of the key marketing messages are delivered at the same time: any USPs the company can claim, reference sites and major customer wins, target market sectors, particular advertising or marketing campaigns, and any competitive knowledge that can help to position you against the competition.

It is also important to keep the sales force aware of any new initiatives the company might be entering into, for example partnerships with another supplier which might make new products available. Additionally, with most companies exploring the Internet as a new channel to market, the impact on the sales force needs to be considered and training provided to ensure that everyone makes the most of this new facility.

Selling skills
This is the area where all sales people need to get off on the right foot if they are not to develop bad habits later on in their career. Traditionally, most companies have provided induction training for their new recruits to ensure that they use the preferred sales methodologies. Companies like Proctor and Gamble, IBM, Digital and Unilever were once recognised as providing some of the best sales training available. Unfortunately, a lot of this has disappeared or become diluted over time and third party training companies have rushed in to fill the gap. This has led to a lack of consistency in that some courses are excellent, many are average, and some are so impractical that they are of no use whatsoever.

However, training in the basics is essential for all new recruits and courses that I would recommend include: SWOT (Strengths, Weaknesses, Opportunities, Threats) Analysis, presentation skills, negotiating skills, time management, account and territory planning, effective questioning and listening skills. Other courses which might be useful if you are involved in selling to large accounts include: solutions selling skills, selling to targeted accounts, managing the complex sale and managing competition and politics.

It is also important to consider training courses tailored for specific markets. These can be quite specialised and are less generally available. I have worked for companies who have created their own such courses by inviting one or two key professionals (often from a customer) or independent consultants to brief the sales team on the unique requirements of a particular market sector. This can be particularly appropriate in business areas where legislation or technical developments are causing profound and rapid change. For example, with the deregulation of old monopoly industries like Telecommunications and Utilities affecting many countries, keeping up with developments can be a full time job. Yet, knowing what is going on (and the implications for doing business) is essential and this can often only be provided by specialist organisations who are closely involved with what is happening.

Business knowledge
General business knowledge can largely be acquired by osmosis, i.e. by soaking up facts and information on an ongoing basis, rather than by sitting down to learn things specifically. The quality TV and radio programmes, newspapers, financial and business journals are all excellent sources of information on business in general, as well as on specific companies and markets. This includes keeping abreast of current affairs on a national as well as global basis. You will also pick up information about your specific markets from your customers,

colleagues and associates, either on a day to day basis or at industry events, conferences or seminars

On a more formal basis, a sales person should be able to read a balance sheet and understand the financial information in a company's report and accounts. A facility with figures is not a prerequisite for a good sales career, but it can help and some basic accountancy skills are invaluable. It can also be useful to have more than a nodding acquaintance with some aspects of the law, especially if it has a particular bearing on your products and services. It is much easier if you understand, even in broad terms, contractual issues, rather than having to keep referring to the company's legal department. And, if customers are starting to take lessons in sales techniques, it might be worth investing in some training on purchasing skills in order to understand the techniques and stratagems professional buyers use.

On a wider basis, there are formal business qualifications which a sales person can pursue, such as an MBA or a Certificate in Management Studies. There are also specific marketing and business degrees and membership of professional bodies and associated examinations which might be useful in some circumstances. None of these is essential to an outstanding sales career, although some top jobs would prefer you to have a degree of some kind or another as proof of your ability to think for yourself and do research effectively. In some cases vocational degrees like Computer Studies can be of benefit if you are specialising in a certain sector.

It is worth mentioning here that basic skills such as computer literacy, a facility with the Internet and an ability to use the most common software applications are all a prerequisite in the modern business environment. I have found that few companies provide training in these areas because they are so ubiquitous that everyone has some ability. However, few people ever use all of the features available to them and often do not make the best use of the ones they think they know.

Never be afraid to ask your IT department for help or to ask colleagues for hints and tips.

How much training, and when, is enough?

This is a difficult question to answer because it depends on so many variables – your experience, market sector, product offerings and so on. Obviously, when you start your career or move to a new job, training is essential in order to get you off on the right foot, but the amount of training each company provides varies so much it is impossible to generalise. In my experience, I have attended an average of one major training course a year – usually a residential course lasting about three days or so – plus a variety of days and half days on specific products or services spread throughout the year. A grand total of between five and seven days per annum. A lot of this has been ad hoc as new products and services have been introduced and there is also 'knowledge transfer' between my colleagues and me as we have gone about our daily business.

As a rough rule of thumb I would suggest that you take whatever training is offered to you by your company so long as it does not have an impact on your day to day job. I know some companies are keen to sponsor key staff through major courses like Marketing Degrees or MBAs, but sales people tend not to fall into this category. And remember you still have a job to do while going through such training, so make sure you can cope with the workload if you are offered the opportunity. Also, companies expect a degree of commitment if they sponsor staff through such courses and you may be tied to that company for a long time if you do not want to repay the course fees.

Training – a personal perspective

When I first started out in sales I was sent on a presentation skills course. I was very nervous and the thought of making a fool of myself in front of my peers was quite daunting. To make matters worse, they videoed everything we did to show us where we were going wrong and what mannerisms we exhibited. I still have the video and had a look at it when I wrote this chapter. I was young! I was also awful, stumbling over my lines, fidgeting, not engaging the audience. But as the course developed I improved. The embarrassment of standing up in front of my colleagues gradually disappeared and I obviously began to feel more comfortable as my body language relaxed and become more engaging. At the end of the course I was still pretty green, but I was infinitely better than when I started and this gave me much more confidence when I had to give my first customer presentation.

10

YOU

What sort of sales person are you?
The sales person is the true value-added ingredient in the sales process. You, personally, make the difference between outstanding success, average performance or failure. It doesn't matter how good your products and services are. A great sales person will be successful even if his offerings are only average, but a poor sales person will fail even if his products are outstanding. Buying and selling are based on communication; on interaction between people. Your customers are really 'buying you' in the first instance. They get an idea about what sort of company you work for and what sort of service they can expect almost as soon as you walk through the door. This can only be reinforced as your relationship with them develops. It is true that first impressions can be wrong, but how much better to make the right impression from the start!

There is a wide range of selling styles – probably as many as there are sales people – but there is a tendency for people to fall into similar categories. Here are some of the types I have met in my career:

1. The hard sell merchant
They are interested in one thing and one thing only – themselves. They are driven to be at the top, regardless of the

cost. They will do whatever is necessary in order to achieve what they want, including the unscrupulous or unethical. They are not interested in what their customers think and will avoid taking responsibility for problems and customer satisfaction. Making the sale and getting the commission is their sole driver. They are invariably successful, especially at winning new business, but at an immense cost in terms of dissatisfied customers, lack of repeat business and poor reputation. Professionalism, regulation and a more aware customer base has helped to curtail hard sell tactics in areas like financial services and home improvements, but they still crop up anywhere where a 'quick buck' can be made at the customer's expense.

2. The soft sell merchant
The complete opposite of the hard sell merchant. They are not driven or aggressive and are overly concerned with being liked. They may never get customer complaints or cancelled business, but they rarely take orders either. They are reluctant to put customers under pressure and have a great deal of difficulty closing business because of this. They try only to do business with people they like and who like them in return and will seek to avoid confrontation, stress, awkward situations and problems. They can make good account managers in certain cases, but they usually tend to move on to careers outside of sales.

3. The order taker
The order taker is getting increasingly scarce today because of competition, but he is still there in certain quarters. The order taker is **not** a sales person and is often characterised by overwhelming arrogance and self regard. He will not exert himself to help customers make a buying decision. If they are not prepared to place an order with him immediately, he isn't going to waste any effort helping them to change their minds

or encourage them to commit quickly. He isn't really interested one way or the other and is little more than an administrator. Order takers were once very common in any sector where business came to them rather than having to go out and find it – car dealerships, estate agencies, retail and so on. Thankfully, a competitive marketplace and more aware customers mean that this breed of non-salesman is diminishing, but they have not disappeared entirely.

I stumbled on a classic example of the 'order taker' when I phoned an estate agent recently. An advert for a property appeared in the local paper under the new instructions section. The estate agent proudly boasted that all three of his offices were open 7 days a week, yet no-one answered the phone at any office on Saturday afternoon. Nor did anyone answer the phone on Sunday morning. There wasn't even an answer phone. I finally spoke to someone on Sunday afternoon who confirmed that they worked half-days at the weekend. "So you are not open seven days a week" I suggested. "So what!" was the reply. On trying to see the property I was informed that the estate agent held the keys and that I could only view the property within office hours. "But I work during the week," I said. "Well you'd better make an appointment for a weekend then and we're already fully booked next Saturday and Sunday." "You don't make it very easy to do business with you," I replied. "That is not our experience. There's been no shortage of interest in the property and we've shown a lot of people over it already," came the smug response. "It has virtually sold itself and we expect several people to make offers."

Such an attitude can only exist when there is a shortage of supply over demand, but will I ever consider that estate agent when it comes to selling my own house? I think not.

4. The average sales person

Most sales people fall into this sort of category, providing a reasonable level of service to their customers and closing an acceptable amount of business. They are comfortable with both new business sales and account management and can close effectively. They are generally professional and are honest and conscientious in their approach. However, while they make a living as sales people, they are rarely at the very top of their game and will seldom over-achieve. They do enough to get by and little more, but probably cannot conceive of the effort needed to be truly outstanding.

5. The top professional

As I said earlier, top professionals comprise about 20% of the sales force and yet they account for something like 80% of the orders taken at any given time (Pareto's Law). They not only provide an all round level of service, they do so outstandingly; going that bit further and spending that bit more effort in ensuring they do their job to the very best of their abilities. It is not enough for them just to get by, they have a need to excel. They are competitive, driven and resilient. Their reputations and their customers are very important to them and customer service, integrity and accountability underpin everything they do.

Presenting yourself professionally

Put yourself in your customers' shoes. They want to see a sales person who gives them a sense of confidence; someone who will take their concerns seriously and really listen to their requirements. Someone who will be able to make valuable recommendations that they can invest in. How you look is the first sign of whether you will match up to these expectations or not. It is not just a matter of avoiding being flashy or scruffy, but of looking the part for the customer you are visiting: of being appropriately dressed. For example, the advertising industry is noted for its casual, but often sophisticated, dress codes. Wearing a suit and tie is not always appropriate, but being professional is a prerequisite if you are to be taken seriously in an industry which is all about image and 'presence'. At the other end of the spectrum, if you sell animal feed directly to farms, wearing a sports jacket, with a pair of wellingtons in the back of the car, is more likely to be appropriate than a pinstripe suit.

Nevertheless, in the United Kingdom at least, a suit and tie is the generally accepted uniform for the professional businessman and a suit with a skirt (rarely trousers) for the professional businesswomen. Sports jackets, trouser suits and 'business casual' can be acceptable in some cases, especially in hot weather, in the office or on training courses, but the trend for 'dress-down' days should be confined to the office only and not for customer meetings. Pride in your appearance is not vanity but a valuable boost to your confidence (the 'look good – feel good' factor), as well as an outward indicator of just how professional you are. Professional does not mean sober or boring, but it probably does mean tasteful, subtle and restrained. It doesn't necessarily mean expensive either, but a really cheap suit will very quickly make you look like a sack of rubbish tied up in the middle!

Avoid bright colours, 'humorous' ties and socks, high fashion items (unless you are in the fashion industry) and unnecessary ornamentation. Have at least two suits to avoid creasing and the material becoming shiny from wear. Make sure your shoes are in good condition and that you clean and polish them regularly, and that your accessories (watches, bags, briefcases, coats, jewellery, make-up, and so on) are appropriate. Keep the use of perfume and aftershave to a minimum and make sure your hair is well groomed. Wear clothes that fit properly and which are comfortable – ill-fitting clothes or shirts that are too tight can easily spoil the image you are trying to create.

Being professional is not just about how you look. What you wear and how you wear it is only part of the story. Presenting yourself professionally applies to anything that affects the image you present to a customer: anything that can reinforce a relaxed, professional and confident image or destroy it if handled poorly. Sales aids and presentation material, your correspondence, proposals and files, even your facility with the social niceties or your sense of humour can fall into this category. Professionalism is a state of mind and it should inform everything you do. I am not suggesting that everything you do should be perfect or overly slick – you are human after all and no-one expects everything to be faultless (and if things are too slick it can be a bit off-putting) – but the image you are trying to portray to your customers is one of quiet confidence. You want them to trust you and you want them to feel that they are in safe hands when dealing with you.

Arriving at a customer's office heavily laden with boxes, samples, folders and bags can easily spoil the calm and professional image you might wish to portray, especially if it all falls in a heap as you attempt to shut the door!

Arriving heavily laden with boxes, samples, folders and bags can easily spoil the calm and professional image.

Arriving late for a meeting immediately gives the wrong impression – punctuality is often a very important measure of how reliable you are. Making sure you are properly prepared is also critical. Senior managers tend to take a very dim view of anyone who has not done his research properly. And your facility with the tools of the trade – presentation equipment or samples for example – gives a customer an impression of what sort of person you are, as well as the company you work for. Even your car will underline your professionalism, especially if you need to chauffeur a prospect to a reference site or take him to lunch. At the very least make sure it is clean and the interior tidy!

Your self image
I have already talked about some of the attributes of professionalism – optimism, confidence, desire, motivation, persistence, enthusiasm and responsibility – but what does this mean for you? Ask yourself, and be honest, how you really see yourself. Physically, do you consider yourself ugly, good-looking or average? Mentally, do you consider yourself clever, stupid, slow to learn or quick to learn? Emotionally, do you consider yourself stable, neurotic, paranoid, immature or mature? Take a good look because the concept or picture that you have of yourself will be the measuring stick that determines how successful you will **allow** yourself to be. It is like a cage or cell you have placed yourself in and it is very hard to escape. People who think they are ugly will often still continue to believe it, even if they have cosmetic surgery to remove the blemishes they considered ugly in the first place. This is because your self-image has nothing to do with your physical appearance or your mental abilities: it consists entirely of the mental picture you have of yourself and once formed it is rarely influenced by what other people say or do. Yet it is a major influence on how you live your life and on how well you can do your job. If you don't like yourself, you will not

present yourself well when dealing with other people. If you feel uncomfortable with yourself, it is likely that when you are with other people – at work or socially – some of this discomfort will communicate itself and they will start to feel awkward in your presence.

Your self image determines what you will allow yourself to achieve. It is formed by conditioning and is sustained by how you think. If you feel in your heart of hearts that you do not deserve to be successful, the effort required to achieve success becomes doubled. Not only do you have to overcome life's own challenges and setbacks, you also have to overcome the drawbacks of your self-image, which, like a ball and chain, will continue to hamper everything you do. That is not to say that a good self image is all about total confidence. Over-confidence and arrogance are not only unattractive, they also have a tendency to blind you to reality and the fact that your abilities may not really be as great as you believe. Everyone has self-doubts and insecurities. This is a fact. Everyone feels unconfident and unsure of themselves at times, but those who are successful work though this. They do not allow self doubt to stop them from getting on with the business of realising their dreams. Their self-image ultimately sees them as successful. They visualise in advance the fact that they will succeed and this feeling is stronger than any self-doubt that might be holding them back.

Your career as a professional sales person
No matter how professional and successful you are, there will be times in your career when you will feel like a change or when circumstances dictate a move to pastures new. I know very few top class sales people who have stayed with the same company all of their working lives. Because they are motivated by new challenges and money, they have a tendency to seek these things out as markets change, adapt and develop – for example, in the software marketplace there has

been a natural migration over the last fifteen years or so from selling relational database management systems (RDBMS) to enterprise resource planning (ERP) to customer relationship management (CRM) and e-Business. The best opportunities and the best commission schemes tend to be found in newly emerging marketplaces because the companies involved need to attract the very best people they can, to get the ball rolling. Once markets begin to mature, things tend to become more bureaucratic and less entrepreneurial – a little less exciting. And commission schemes likewise become less generous as time goes by!

The most effective way of securing a new position is via your network of contacts and colleagues. If your peers acknowledge you as good, you will never want for employment opportunities. After all, they already know what you have done, what you are capable of, how you work and what sort of person you are. If managers move on to pastures new, they like to take their old team with them if it has been particularly successful – you often see the same faces cropping up in new companies every few years or so as better opportunities present themselves and whole teams move *en masse*.

If you are thinking about moving, job advertisements in the quality press may look enticing, especially given some of the salaries quoted. But many jobs so advertised are filled before the paper even comes out! In many cases press ads of this kind attract literally hundreds of applications and the people administering the response will be ruthless in rejecting anything that, even slightly, misses their base specification. They are looking for no more than five to ten top class candidates to put in front of their customer. Anything else will be rejected. Increasingly, they use computer systems to vet CVs, searching on key words in the text to 'prove' your eligibility for a specific job. If your CV lacks one or more of these key words, it will be discarded. In some cases recruitment consultants run attractive adverts, not because there is a specific vacancy they are trying to fill for a customer, but because they are looking to build up a pool of suitable candidates who they can then market onwards.

By the way, your Curriculum Vitae is a very important document and it makes sense to keep it up to date on a regular basis. Not because you are mercenary and always on the look out for a new or better position, but because it is an important record of your career and it needs to reflect your latest successes and experience. There is plenty of advice around on how to prepare a CV and I don't propose to dwell on it here, but it should be clear, concise and any achievements made supported by evidence. It should also be fairly short, certainly no more than three pages maximum and your latest experience should be at the top.

Recruitment consultants

Another source of employment options is through recruitment consultants. At their best, recruitment consultants – executive search and selection, headhunters, human resourcing, placement consultants, call them what you will – can provide an excellent service, matching your particular requirements to specific jobs or companies. They often handle recruitment on behalf of several companies and know of vacancies which are never published or advertised. They will normally find two or three people who closely fit the job specification or brief and won't waste anyone's time by parading hoards of unsuitable candidates in front of the client. They do what they say they will do and they expect you to do the same. They will provide accurate feedback on your performance at interview and they will expect you to listen to it. At their worst, recruitment consultants are a nightmare, forever badgering you, using silly subterfuges, ruses and tricks to find out names and phone numbers. They often refuse to tell you the name of the company they are recruiting for – mainly because there isn't one and all they are doing is trying to find a good candidate who might be interested in moving and who they can then market onwards.

If you are even remotely good at your job, you will be approached by recruitment consultants at some time. There is a shortage of skilled sales people in the marketplace and your name will end up on a recruitment consultant's computer, whether it is from word of mouth or through a recruitment exercise the consultant undertakes. The first you will know of it is when you get a phone call saying something like: "Hello Mr. Sheppard, this is John Smith here. Your name has been brought to my attention and I was wondering if now was a good time to talk about your career aspirations". How you deal with such calls will depend on how happy you are with your current job, how professional the recruiter is – it can be very interesting to be on the receiving end of a serious sales pitch! – and what opportunity you are being considered for. If you say no, the first thing you will be asked for are the names of anyone you might recommend in your stead! If you say yes, you will have to attend an interview with the consultants before you ever get to meet their client and it quite likely that there will be at least two if not three or four client interviews to attend before a decision is finally made.

As part of the interview process, you may be asked to complete a series of Psychometric tests. These are designed to try and ascertain your psychological profile – how you think, how you sell, how you cope in pressurised situations and so on. It is claimed that you cannot fudge your answers to give a particular result. They are a hurdle you have to complete if the job is one you want. Psychometric tests were very popular a few years ago and, although still used quite a lot today, they are not quite as ubiquitous. It is unlikely that such a test will be used exclusively in deciding whether you are right for a job. You will still have to go to interviews and people will still make judgments and decisions on a personal basis. But, if you are a borderline candidate and there is some doubt as to your suitability, the test will be used to help make the final decision.

Never pay for recruitment services. Recruitment consultants are paid anything from 20% to 100% of a job's salary as a fee for finding the right person to fill the vacancy. There are several executive search companies who masquerade as careers consultants, and who charge you for their services as well as gaining a fee from their clients for filling vacancies – beware of anyone who asks for money for finding you employment.

Money

Financial reward is a key driver for most sales people. Because selling can be such a high pressure environment, the temptation to 'work hard/play hard' can be overwhelming. Letting off steam is no bad thing, but frittering away your hard earned commission on the fleeting and ephemeral is not sensible in the long run. I know it is boring talking about pension schemes, tax and savings, but in a sales career, no matter how successful you are, money does not come in on a regular basis. Obviously, your basic salary is paid monthly, but your commission will only be paid once you have sold something and this can mean serious peaks and troughs in your income. This is of even greater importance if you work on commission only. Putting something aside to smooth out these irregularities and to accommodate an anticipated 'rainy day' is not just common sense, it is a necessity if you wish to avoid straitened circumstances when sales are slow.

I know some sales managers who like to employ sales people who have a few financial difficulties on the basis that their problems will drive them to achieve more and quickly – a large mortgage, a taste for the finer things in life, expensive hobbies – all can contribute. I do not see this as a sensible policy. If a sales person is desperate because he needs the money, there will be a tendency for him to be unethical. He will want to take business no matter what the cost because of this desperation. He is unlikely to be particularly careful or fastidious about where the business comes from, or how he goes about acquiring it. In my experience, the best sales people are highly motivated anyway. They do not need some artificial stimulus to drive them on. They may be motivated by money, but they are not desperate for it, so they are under no additional pressures as they go about their jobs.

Make sure that you do not find yourself in financial difficulties. I am not advocating a monastic lifestyle because enjoying the fruits of your labours is one of the reasons for doing a high pressure, high reward job in the first place. But, making sure you take care of the basics first of all isn't just common sense, it is part of being professional. You will provide your customers with a better service, and reduce your personal pressures considerably, if your have your finances under control.

11

SUMMARY

Selling is a professional career, one which can bring great rewards and satisfaction. But, whether you wish to pursue selling as a career for yourself or to improve your sales effectiveness within your own profession, the skills that make the best sales people the very best can be identified and practised.

This book has been my attempt, after nearly twenty years in the business, to highlight where top professionals 'gain an edge' and, in summary, here are the key elements which I believe to be the basis of success:

1. Start off on the right foot. Only practising the right way to do things makes perfect.
2. Do not become obsolete – either through lack of training or ill-health. Invest in yourself.
3. Professionalism is a state of mind. Practise it at all times.
4. Treat your customers the same way you like to be treated.
5. Plan to be successful, but put in the effort to ensure it. Never take no for an answer.
6. Believe in yourself, like yourself, sell yourself. You are the most important USP of all.
7. Selling is a people business. Work with them for mutual benefit.

8.   Listen and learn – knowledge and understanding are the basis of success.
9.   Be accountable. Honesty, integrity, responsibility and trust are the cornerstones of professionalism.
10. Enjoy what you do warts and all. Optimism and enthusiasm should underpin everything you do.
11. Never accept second best – either from others or from yourself.
12. Never stop prospecting and use everything available to you to achieve success. There are no limitations.

INDEX

FREE
If you would like an up-to-date list of all **RIGHT WAY** titles currently available, please send a stamped self-addressed envelope to ELLIOT RIGHT WAY BOOKS, LOWER KINGSWOOD, TADWORTH, SURREY, KT20 6TD, U.K. or visit our web site at www.right-way.co.uk